THE
DRIVING
TEST
IN
IRELAND
New Edition

GW00367032

DES CUMMINS

BLACKWATER PRESS

Produced by Blackwater Press
Broomhill Business Park, Tallaght, Dublin 24.

©1996 Blackwater Press
First published in 1992
Second Edition 1996
ISBN 0 86121 804 3

Editor
HILDA O'SULLIVAN

Design and Layout
PHILIP RYAN/PAULA BYRNE

Illustration
CAROL KEARNS

The greatest care has been taken in the publication of this book. However, neither the author nor the publishers can accept responsibility for any errors or misinterpretation which may occur, or their consequences.

It should be noted that the Rules and Road Regulations may change from time to time. Every effort has been made to give the correct information at the time of publication.

About the Author

The author of this book has been actively involved in the driving tuition industry for many years. He has undergone various examinations: an exam for the Motor Schools Association of Ireland, followed by a diploma from the same association, and another from the RACRI (Royal Automobile Association Registered Instructor). He is a member of the I.D.I.A. (Irish Driving Instructors Association), formerly the A.D.I.R.

As secretary of Registration for the M.S.A.I. (Motor Schools Association of Ireland) he has been involved in the formation of the new Driving Instructors Register of Ireland (D.I.R.). He has held the position of Chairman and European Representative for the M.S.A.I.

For his services to the industry, he has been honoured with a prestigious accolade from the Master Tutors of Driving (G.B.) M. Inst., MTD, Acc.

He is currently executive chairman of the Driving Instructors Register of Ireland (DIR).

Acknowledgements

To my two sons, Alan and Matthew.

My thanks go to the editor, Hilda O'Sullivan, whose help was much appreciated. Many thanks to Lorraine Madden for the typing and retyping of this book.

I wish to acknowledge the assistance given by the following: The National Safety Council, Dublin Road Safety Council, Department of the Environment (Driver Testing), Dublin Corporation Motor Tax Office and FÁS, the Training and Employment Authority.

I wish to thank the committee of the Motor Schools Association of Ireland especialy Mr Bernard Shiel, Standards and Training Officer whose help and assistance was much appreciated.

My appreciation must also go to Mr Brian M. Weeks D.O.T. A.D.I. UK Consultant to the Driving Instructor Register of Ireland, Ltd.

Des Cummins ADIA. MSAI. IDIA, RACRI,
M. DIR, M. INST, M.T.D. ACC.

Contents

Introduction

The need for this revised edition of *The Driving Test in Ireland* has arisen from the success of the first edition and from the many new requirements for the 1996 Driving Test, which have been implemented because of Article 10 of EC Directive 80/1263 which aims to have a standardised test for Europe. This involves a more detailed knowledge of the workings of the vehicle and a written theory test, along with the traditional practical test. For the theory test, the author has also written *The Theory Questions & Answers Book* which should be studied in conjunction with this book. A thorough knowledge of the *Rules of the Road* is also essential.

However, the most important guarantee of success in the driving test is a registered driving instructor namely registered instructors of DIR, Driving Instructor Register of Ireland, MSAI, Motor Schools Association of Ireland, IDIA, Irish Driving Instructors Association. Learning to drive is a life skill, a skill that will keep you and your passengers safe, and give you enough confidence to handle any traffic situation you may come across. He/she will not only teach you the art of good driving but will entrust you with a life skill. Safe driving is about attitude, attitude to other road users. Human error is the cause of 9 out of 10 accidents.

The aim of this book is to dispel some of your fears of the Driving Test. We will take the test step by step, expand your knowledge and build up your confidence. We also hope to play down some of the myths surrounding the Driving Test e.g. fail/pass quotas etc... Preparation is the key word. The purpose of this book is not to replace the *Rules of the Road*, an official booklet from the Department of the Environment which we strongly recommend you read, nor is it intended to replace professional tuition. The purpose is to complement these sources of knowledge and to have you well-prepared and confident for your Driving Test.

All About The Driving Test

REQUIREMENTS FOR UNDERGOING YOUR DRIVING TEST

☐ **1.** Take along a valid Irish provisional licence for the category of the driving test you are now undergoing.

☐ **2.** Your vehicle must be in roadworthy condition, with lights, brakes and signals, etc. in working order.

☐ **3.** Your vehicle must display a current tax disc with proper registration number shown.

☐ **4.** Your vehicle must display a valid insurance disc (if Irish registered) with registration number, not chassis number, shown.

☐ **5.** L plates (15 cm²) with a red L on a white background should be displayed front and rear of all vehicles except motorbikes and tractors.

☐ **6.** You are only allowed to cancel a driving test application twice for any one application, otherwise you forfeit your fee and must re-apply and return to the end of the queue. (See letter on page 15).

Conditions one to five are legal requirements. Failing any of these, your driving test will not be conducted and you will lose your fee and go back to the end of the waiting list.

Please note that your driving examiner is exempt from wearing a seat belt (if he/she so wishes), do not insist on him/her wearing it.

Also note that if either tax or insurance disc is faded or illegible, you must have them replaced prior to the test. Trade plates are not acceptable for undergoing your test.

Use the boxes provided on page 9 to tick off requirements several days before your test, thus giving you the time to have everything in order for the day.

N.B. If you have just realised that **your provisional licence is out of date** for the day of your test, you will need to have it replaced. This procedure is not as simple as it used to be. Driving licences or provisional licences are not handed out over the counter as was the practice previously. Now you must receive your documents through the post. In some areas this may take several weeks. However, if your driving test is imminent, you should bring your driving test appointment slip and a completed provisional licence form, not forgetting two photographs, to your relevant licencing authority, and see the supervisor in charge. He/she will normally issue your licence within a couple of hours. Note that the licence application, depending on your category, may require general medical information. You may use the Form D501, available through your local tax office, and have it completed and signed by your general practitioner. Persons over the age of 70 will also need this certificate of fitness (D501).

Eyesight Test: All applicants for a provisional licence for categories A1, A, B, EB or W must undergo a once-off eyesight test. If your optician has stated that you must wear corrective lenses, you should not forget them for the test, or indeed ever drive without them as this may invalidate your insurance cover should you be involved in an accident. This information is recorded on your licence with the words, " corrective lenses must be worn."

Medical Test: Applicants for a provisional licence for categories C, C1, D, D1, EC, EC1, ED or ED1 must undergo a medical examination.

Special Driving Tests: Candidates applying for a driving test, who have any disability (difficulty of hearing or any other physical disability) should have their practitioner fill out the Form D501, Certificate of Fitness. It would also be courteous to include any detail they might find informative to the Department, e.g. any special adaptations to the vehicle they propose to use for the driving test. These should be attached and sent to:

The Driver Testing Section, Department of the Environment, Government Offices, Ballina, Co.Mayo. Phone: 096-70677

If you have any special queries regarding your particular disability, you should write to or phone the above address.

Driving Tuition for the Disabled

All relevant information may be had from the Irish Wheelchair Association, Aras Chuchulan, Blackheath Drive, Clontarf, Dublin 3. Tel. 01 8338241/8335366.

AN SCRÚDÚ TIOMÁNAÍOCHTA

(The Driving Test *in Irish*)

In order to undergo the theory or practical driving test through the Irish language you must fill out a special form, available through your local Motor Taxation Office. Your tests will then be conducted through Irish. There is also a special form for those wishing to have their Driving Licence document in Irish. To obtain these forms you should contact your local Taxation Office.

GENERAL CATEGORIES

Detailed description of categories of vehicles for the Driving Licence Application Form:

Category	Vehicle
A1	Motorcycles under 125cc, with or without sidecar
A	Motorcycles with or without sidecar
B	Vehicles with passenger accommodation for 8 persons or less and with a design g.v.w. not over 3,500kg
C1	Vehicles with passenger accommodation for 8 persons or less and with a design g.v.w. over 3,500kg but not over 7,500kg
C	Vehicles with passenger accommodation for 8 persons or less and with a design g.v.w. over 3,500kg
D1	Vehicles with passenger accommodation for more than 8 persons but not more than 16 persons
D	Vehicles with passenger accommodation for more than 8 persons
EB	Vehicles in category B with a trailer attached
EC1	Vehicles in category C1 with a trailer attached
EC	Vehicles in category C with a trailer attached
ED1	Vehicles in category D1 with a trailer attached
ED	Vehicles in category D with a trailer attached
W	Work vehicle and land tractors, with or without a trailer attached

"*Passenger accommodation*" means seating accommodation in addition to the driver.

"*Design g.v.w.*" means design gross vehicle weight i.e. the design laden weight.

Accompanying driver

A provisional licence holder should be accompanied by a full licence holder when driving. However, this is not necessary during the second licence. Check the conditions on your licence or with your motor taxation office. The carrying of any passengers on motorcycles driven by a provisional licence holder is prohibited (see page 108).

List of categories and their requirements for the Driving Test and Minimum Age Requirement

Category	Type of vehicle required for the purpose of a Driving Test
A	*18 years* Two wheeled Motorcycles with an engine capacity of at least 150 cubic centimetres.
A1	*16 years* Two wheeled Motorcycles with an engine capacity not exceeding 125 cubic centimetres.
B	*17 years* Four wheeled vehicles (Motor Cars and Light Vans) having a design gross vehicle weight not exceeding 3,500kg and having passenger accommodation for not more than 8 persons.
C	*18 years* Vehicles (Trucks) having a design gross vehicle weight of at least 9,500 kg, a wheelbase of at least 3.75 metres and passenger accommodation for not more than 8 persons.
C1	*18 years* Vehicles (Light Trucks and Vans) having a design gross vehicle weight exceeding 3,500 kg but not exceeding 7,500 kg and having passenger accommodation for not more than 8 persons.
D	*21 years* Vehicles (Buses) having passenger accommodation for at least 28 persons, an overall length of at least 9 metres and an overall width of approximately 2.5 metres.

D1 *21 years* Vehicles (Minibuses) with passenger accommodation for more than 8 persons but not more than 16 persons and whose overall length is not more than 6 metres.

EC *18 years* Articulated Trucks having an overall length of at least 12 metres.

Note: Tests carried out in vehicles with automatic transmission

Persons undergoing a driving test in an automatic vehicle will receive a restricted certificate of competency, that is to say, they may only drive a vehicle with automatic transmission in that category. Ignoring this fact would mean breaking the law and may invalidate your insurance. The same applies to persons who have undergone a driving test in a specially adapted vehicle to suit a particular physical disability of the licensee.

APPOINTMENT FOR PRACTICAL DRIVING TEST

Along with your driving test appointment slip you should receive a booklet entitled *Preparing For Your Driving Test.* You should read it carefully.

ENVIRONMENT

Reference No.: ....

(Please quote above Ref. in all correspondence)

DEPARTMENT OF
THE ENVIRONMENT

AN ROINN
COMHSHAOIL

GOVERNMENT
OFFICES

BALLINA, CO. MAYO

OIFIGÍ RIALTAIS

BÉAL AN ÁTHA

CO. MHAIGH EO

TEL 096 70677

FAX 096 70680

GTN 7 96 I

Dear Sir/Madam,

I wish to acknowledge receipt of your recent application and fee (non refundable) for a driving test in Category B (Motor Car/Light Van). Notification of an appointment for your test will be issued to you in due course.

At this stage you should note carefully the following.
1. You must provide the vehicle for the test.
2. If the vehicle you intend to use is automatic or semi-automatic, this fact will be noted on your Certificate of Competency should you pass your driving test, and you will only be licenced to drive such vehicles.
3. On the day of your test you will be required to produce a current Irish Provisional Licence for the above category. In the event that your licence will expire in the near future you should apply for a renewal in advance, as a delay of 3/4 weeks can occur in issuing renewals.
4. Eligibility for a third or subsequent provisional licence for any category of vehicle is dependent on you having undergone a driving test within the previous two years. If you have a doubt about your eligibility for any Provisional Licence you should enquire with your local Motor Taxation Office.
5. A limit of two cancellations applies to appointments issued on foot of this application.

Please note that the new edition of the Rules of the Road is available at Post Offices.

Yours faithfully,

15

On the Day of the Test

Understandably, on the day of your Driving Test, you will be nervous. The main thing to remember is that your examiner is just doing a job and all he or she wishes to see is a proficient standard of driving.

By the time you have reached your driving test date, you will have heard many alarming stories e.g. quotas, end of week tests never pass, end of month tests ditto, Friday afternoon tests much the same, or what about Monday morning tests?... These stories are simply not true. If you have received professional tuition and have attained the standard required, you should pass.

Remember, it goes without saying, the more training you have, provided by a professional instructor teaching you a more relaxed approach and attitude to driving, the more competent you should feel on the day of your test. As for realistic mock tests, you should arrange with your driving instructor to have a pre-test professionally conducted like an examiner, thus giving you a true feeling for the test on the day.

It may be appropriate to mention at this stage, that if a fault in the vehicle is the reason for the driving test not taking place, you will lose your fee.

If, however, your examiner does not turn up for your test, due to illness for example, you will have recourse through the Department and a new appointment will be made.

A further note: it is a criminal offence to attempt to bribe an examiner in any way.

Category B Test Content

It is advisable to relax for a short period of time before driving again after your test

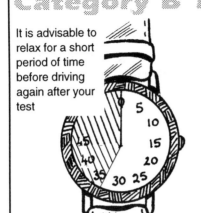

ARRIVE 5 MINUTES PRIOR TO YOUR TEST

Administration
Move to car
Cockpit drill
Move away
Drive
Light traffic
Turnabout
Right and left corners
Hill starts
Drive
Road and lane position
Roundabouts

Reverse into a limited opening
Hand/arm signals
Drive
Use of controls
Lane Discipline
Drive
Use of mirrors
Overtaking
Use of speed
Use of signals
Parking

Approach to junctions
One way systems
General observation
Driver attitude
Start of return to test centre
Drive
Road markings
Yield and stop signs
Traffic lights and filter systems
Overall Proficiency
General handling of the vehicle

This list illustrates some of the exercises a candidate would have to demonstrate to an examiner during a typical Category B practical driving test though not necessarily in this sequence.

PRACTICAL DRIVING TEST

Knowledge, skill and behaviour for driving a power driven vehicle is required under Article 10 of Directive 80/1263 EC.

You will be tested on all aspects of your driving. In order to drive safely, a driver must have a sound knowledge and understanding of the following:

1. handling the vehicle safely
2. recognising all impending traffic dangers ahead and around the vehicle
3. understanding and acting upon all traffic signs
4. having sufficient control of the vehicle not to create dangerous situations
5. reacting to any situations caused by others
6. complying with road traffic regulations
7. being able to detect any major technical faults within the vehicle
8. knowing the factors affecting driver behaviour e.g. alcohol, fatigue, poor eyesight, the use of drugs, prescribed or otherwise, etc.

STEP BY STEP THROUGH THE TEST

The diagram on page 17 shows the main points an examiner looks out for. The sequences listed are not necessarily in order as it will depend on the examiner and the direction he chooses to take. However, it may be used as a guide to the amount you will have to do on the day.

The list on page 17 is based on a category B driving test (see page 12) which lasts about 25 minutes. Other categories may well last longer (see HGV, page 111).

Do not overlook the minutes of relaxation after your driving test as you will have been stressed throughout that period. Rest for several minutes before returning to the road. This will have a calming down effect immediately after your test.

You should note your legal position pertaining to the rules of the road when in control of a mechanically propelled vehicle. Present Irish law clearly states that the holder of a Provisional Licence or Learner's Permit should not drive unsupervised on their first and third or indeed any subsequent provisional licence. A Provisional Licence or Learner's Permit lasts for two years. The legal position also states that a person on a second Provisional Licence may drive unsupervised and as such would be able to present themselves for a driving test without being accompanied by an experienced licence holder in the category of test being conducted.

General procedure on the day of the test

Arrive at the test centre prior to your appointed time. You should wait in the waiting room. Your name will be called in due course by your examiner.

The exam will start after you produce your current Irish Provisional Licence to the examiner and sign the required administration forms including a Declaration of Road Worthiness and Insurance (see page 20).

You will then accompany the examiner to the vehicle where he/she will check your tax and insurance disc and inspect your L plates (front and rear) and generally check the condition of your vehicle. In the case of a HGV, the examiner will check the lights, indicators, stop lights and generally all electrics, not forgetting the minimum number of mirrors, one left and one right. Before moving away, your examiner will say words to this effect: "There should be no further conversation in the vehicle between you and me other than to tell you to turn right or left. In the absence of a right or a left, I would like you to assume straight. If, however, you don't understand, you may ask and I will repeat." Don't be unduly worried about this, as it is all part of the test. Try not to be put off by his/her presence in the vehicle. Your examiner may take notes during the course of your driving test. Do not be alarmed at this as it is normal procedure. If you show that you are a competent and confident driver, you should pass your test. Remember your training!

DECLARATION OF ROADWORTHINESS AND INSURANCE

Department of the Environment
An Roinn Comhshaoil

Government Offices,
Ballina,
Co. Mayo.

Telephone: (096)-70677
Fax: (096)-70680

Oifigí Rialtais,
Béal an Átha,
Co. Mhaigh Eo.

DECLARATION OF ROADWORTHINESS AND INSURANCE

Reference Number - _____

The vehicle I am providing for my test is in roadworthy condition and I am properly insured to drive it in a public place during the course of my driving test.

Signed _____

Date _____

D.T. (B) 11/90

He/she will ask you to move away and take whatever direction the examiner has planned. For the most part, a high percentage of examiners will ask you to do a turnabout as a first manoeuvre, followed shortly by a reverse into a limited opening on the left. This is almost certainly followed by arm/handsignals and finally a hill start. This may not be the exact sequence in your test centre, as this will depend on the number of examiners working from the test centre on that day and on any obstructions and traffic within the areas intended for your manoeuvres.

Your test route will be a well balanced drive of about five miles under a variety of road and traffic conditions which will include moving away, right turns, left turns, driving along main roads, emerging at junctions, traffic lights, use of traffic lanes, road position, use of controls, mirrors and signals. And remember general observation will play a very big part in your test.

Almost before you know it, you will be on the way back to the test centre. You will have been concentrating so much, you will wonder where the time went!

Examiners are not normally allowed to speak to you during your test. Most examiners will not do so. This is because it is felt that it would impair your concentration. In fact, many an examiner has been reprimanded for trying to calm a person down or for trying to help them relax. Complaints have been known to be made when such situations have occurred, this is why the rule now rigidly applies.

On your return to the test centre, you will accompany the examiner into the centre where you will be informed whether you gained your Certificate of Competency or not. Examiners are not allowed to discuss the reasons for failing. Should you be unfortunate enough to fail your driving test you will be given a form entitled "Refusal to gain a Certificate of Competency", along with a detailed list of the areas where you were deficient in the minimum standard required to pass your driving test. You will also be given a four page document entitled *The Driving Test*. If you have taken professional driving tuition, you should now return to your registered driving instructor and ask for a detailed explanation on the points identified by your examiner, as the Department of the Environment will not allow the examiner to explain his markings. An examiner's decision is final. All driving testers are trained to the same standard and have regular checks by their respective supervisory examiners. In the interest of fairness it is for this reason that you may have a supervisor tester travel with you on your test. He will not be testing you, but your examiner. The supervisory tester would not influence the decision reached by your appointed examiner.

If you have not taken professional tuition before you should now contact a registered driving instructor for professional tuition before applying for a further test. At this point it should be mentioned that a high percentage of failures are due to three main reasons:

1. faults relating to vehicle control and road procedure
2. lack of professional tuition
3. incorrect observation

Remember, nerves alone should not bring about a refusal of a Certificate of Competency.

The Theory Test

Study this book *The Driving Test in Ireland*, *The Theory Questions and Answers Book* and the *Rules of the Road* which is issued by the National Safety Council.

The contents of this government handbook will be tested in a separate theory test conducted by the Department of the

Environment (Driver Testing Section). It is indeed recommended that a person who has passed the driving test should periodically read the latest editions, as new laws, regulations and EC directives are introduced all the time.

Questions for the Theory Test will be in a multiple choice format at a separate time to the practical test. The questions will be posed in written form, with three or indeed in some cases four answers given, you simply have to mark the right one. The European Council directive on driving licences for all of Europe (91/493/EEC) has set the minimum requirements for driving tests. These must consist of:

1. a theory test
2. a test of skills and behaviour.

A key factor in answering any question on the *Rules of the Road* would be to think of the safety aspect first. Although this book refers a lot to the "Driving test", it must go without saying that "test standard" is a good standard to maintain for the rest of your life. Never think, "I have to drive like this for a test" and the next day forget all you have been taught. Your life could depend on the good habits acquired under the guidance of your driving instructor!

One must remember that test standard is a minimum standard and that over the next number of years you will still be gaining experience. You will only be commencing a learning process that will take a lifetime. After passing the driving test, consideration should be given to night time lessons, motorway lessons, advanced and defensive driving courses. These courses are generally undertaken by your Registered Instructor (RDI).

Theory Questionnaire

1. **Q.** What shape and colour is a warning sign?
   A. Diamond shape - yellow and black.
2. **Q.** What is the law for drivers and front seat passengers?
   A. They must wear a seat belt.
3. **Q.** What are the main causes of skidding?
   A. Driving too fast for the conditions - harsh braking - improper use of gears - harsh acceleration - wet/greasy/icy surfaces - improper use of steering.
4. **Q.** When should you not drive?
   A. Under the influence of alcohol, drugs (prescribed or otherwise), or when tired or drowsy.
5. **Q.** What should always be kept clean on your vehicle?
   A. Lights - Reflectors - Windows - Mirrors - Registration plate.
6. **Q.** What is the rule about passing animals on the road?
   A. Slow down, give plenty of room, do not sound your horn or rev your engine. Have patience.
7. **Q.** Can you reverse from a minor road to a major road?
   A. No. (You should only reverse from a major road to a minor road.)
8. **Q.** What shape is the sign that regulates?
   A. Regulatory signs are round with red on white background with the exception of three: stop, yield and end of speed limit.
9. **Q.** When should you use your hazard warning lights?
   A. When your car is broken down, or at any hazardous situation where it would be beneficial to other road users, or at the scene of an accident.

10. Q. What vehicles are prohibited from using a motorway?

A. Learner driver vehicles, motorbikes under 50cc, invalid cars or horsedrawn vehicles, or any vehicles not capable of attaining 30 mph.

11. Q. What should a broken white line mean to you?

A. A broken white line divides the centre of the road and should only be crossed if safe or necessary to do so.

12. Q. What is the sequence of traffic lights?

A. Green - Amber - Red - Green.

13. Q. How far from a junction is it safe to park?

A. 120 feet (15 feet - legal requirement).

14. Q. What is the rule on entering a roundabout?

A. Give way to traffic on your immediate right.

15. Q. What are three lanes on a motorway for?

A. Lefthand lanes are for driving in, middle and righthand lanes are for overtaking only.

16. Q. Name some places where you should not overtake.

A. Where you cannot see far enough ahead - a humpback bridge - too close to junctions - corners - pedestrian crossing - hatchmarkings - over a continuous white line.

17. Q. Name some places where you should not park.

A. Too close to a junction - opposite a stationary vehicle - corners - double yellow lines - single yellow lines (within time zones) - opposite a continuous white line.

18. Q. What is a hard shoulder for?

A. Emergencies or breakdowns only.

19. Q. What is the overall stopping distance at:

(a) 30 mph?

(b) 40 mph?

(c) 50 mph?

A. (a) 75ft approx.

(b) 120ft approx.

(c) 175 ft approx.

20. Q. What do the *Rules of the Road* say about sounding your horn?

A. You should not sound your horn between the hours of 23.30 and 7.00, except in emergencies.

21. Q. To keep your vehicle in legal condition, what should you pay particular attention to?

A. Brakes ^{2}lights -^{3}tyres ^{4}steering -^{5}indicators -^{6}wipers ^{7}speedometer ^{8}horn -^{9}silencer.

22. Q. What are the minimum lighting requirements on your vehicle?

A. A motor vehicle (except a motor-cycle) must be equipped with two headlights (white or yellow),^{2}two white sidelights (front),^{3}two red rear lights,^{4}two red stoplights at rear,^{5}two red rear reflectors,^{6}number plate lighting to the rear and^{7}directional indicators, front and rear.

23. Q. What does an amber traffic light mean?

A. Stop, if safe to do so.

24. Q. How should you approach a green light that has been green from the first time you have seen it?

A. Approach with caution at a speed which would enable you to stop safely if necessary, preferably in 3rd gear or lower.

25. Q. Name some ways you may be marked for coasting.

A. You may be marked for coasting if you are travelling with ^{1}your clutch depressed for a distance greater than necessary, or by^{2}selecting neutral gear prior to stopping, or by^{3}selecting gear and holding your clutch in the disengaged position while the main braking is being undertaken and only then releasing the clutch.

26. Q. What should you do before moving off?
 A. Check your mirror(s), signal and check your blind spots.
27. Q. In what position should you drive?
 A. As close as practicable to the left.
28. Q. Which is the safest way to park your vehicle at night?
 A. Passenger side to kerb, reflectors to the following traffic.
29. Q. What should you do if dazzled by oncoming lights at night?
 A. Look to the left, do not look directly at the oncoming lights, slow down and stop if necessary.
30. Q. What is the first thing you should do after being involved in an accident?
 A. Stop.
31. Q. What side of the road should your passengers alight from, especially children?
 A. Pavement side.
32. Q. If a blind person was crossing the road, how would you know he/she was deaf as well?
 A. There would be two reflective bands on his/her white stick.
33. Q. When may you overtake on the left?
 A. When the driver in front of you has signalled his intention to turn right; in a one way street; in slow moving traffic where the lefthand lane is moving faster than the righthand lane; in a lefthand filterlane.
34. Q. What is the rule about yellow box junctions?
 A. Do not enter box unless your **exit road** is clear except on turning right and you are only prevented by oncoming traffic.

35. Q. What do zig-zag lines mean on approach to a zebra crossing?

A. No overtaking, no parking, no stopping (except for traffic reasons).

36. Q. Give some examples of places where you should be more aware of pedestrians?

A. ¹Corners -²traffic lights -³junctions -⁴bus stops -⁵when overtaking parked cars or lorries -⁶around ice cream vans - near schools, etc.

37. Q. If you were driving along the road and felt drowsy what should you do?

A. Open your window, pull over and stop.

38. Q. At a pelican crossing what does a flashing amber mean?

A. Proceed with caution if no pedestrian is crossing.

39. Q. When should you use your lights during daylight hours?

A. ¹During poor visibility, ²falling snow and ³in fog.

40. Q. What is the minimum legal thread depth on a tyre?

A. 1.6mm.

41. Q. How many types of pedestrian crossings are there?

A. Two, controlled and uncontrolled.

42. Q. How would you describe an uncontrolled pedestrian crossing?

A. Flashing beacons and black and white road markings and in some cases zig-zag lines.

43. Q. What is a controlled pedestrian crossing?

A. Pedestrian traffic lights.

44. Q. What road markings are you likely to find at traffic lights?

A. ¹Stop line -²two pedestrian lines -³two yellow lines - ⁴continuous white line -⁵yellow box -⁶directional arrows.

45. Q. What road signs would you expect to see approaching a major road?

A. Warning sign: major road ahead. Regulatory sign: yield or stop.

46. Q. What road markings would you expect to see prohibiting you from entering a one way street?

A. A continuous white line painted across the road, backed by a broken white line, also a NO ENTRY sign.

47. Q. Why is a stop sign or a yield sign so shaped?

A. If defaced in any way, the driver recognises the shape.

48. Q. What are chevrons?

A. They are directional arrows to indicate deviation ahead, bad bends, etc.

49. Q. On your driving test, while doing your turnabout, must the manoeuvre be done in three movements?

A. No. It is called a turnabout, not a 'three point turn'.

50. Q. How many types of road signs are there?

A. Five: informative (information signs), warning (black diamond shape), regulatory (round), motorway (blue & white) and orange (roadworks).

51. Q. Which control makes the car move off?

A. The clutch.

52. Q. Where would parking obscure the view of others?

A. At junctions, on a bend or brow of a hill, on the approach side of a zebra crossing, etc.

53. Q. What is the minimum insurance on a vehicle?

A. Third party.

54. Q. Name some signs and road markings which would prohibit you from parking.

A. No parking signs, clearway signs, bus lane signs, yellow lines or continuous white line in the centre of the road.

55. Q. When is it particularly dangerous to park on the road at night?

    A. In fog.

56. Q. What lights should you drive on in fog?

    A. Dipped headlights.

57. Q. What must you make sure of before starting to reverse?

    A. That you have a clear view and that no pedestrians, especially children, are crossing behind your vehicle. Look out for cyclists.

58. Q. How do you approach and take the third exit off an ordinary four road roundabout?

    A. You must mirror, signal right and manoeuvre right (just left of centre) on approach. Maintain your signal until you reach the exit before the one you want to take, then you must check your mirror and change your signals to the left, manoeuvre left and exit.

59. Q. How should you take the second exit off a roundabout assuming the second exit is directly ahead?

    A. Drive in on the left handside, no signal until you pass the first exit, then signal left.

60. Q. What must you remember before you overtake?

    A. Clear view ahead and M.S.M.M. (mirror, signal, mirror, manoeuvre).

61. Q. What do you do on approaching a junction to turn left/right if there are pedestrians already crossing?

    A. Allow them to cross.

62. Q. On a roundabout with only three exits, how would you approach and signal taking the second exit assuming the exit is to the right?

    A. If the second exit is past 12 o'clock on a clock face, approach and signal exactly like a third exit.

63. Q. Name some conditions that would increase your braking distance.

A. Rain (road wet after a dry spell), ice, snow, fallen leaves, loose chippings, worn tyres, etc.

64. Q. What is the significance of a driver flashing his/her lights at you?

A. Take note of his presence.

65. Q. What does a green light mean?

A. Proceed with caution if your way ahead is clear.

66. Q. What is the national speed limit?

A. 60mph, 96kph.

67. Q. What vehicles must you give way to at a junction of equal importance?

A. All vehicles approaching from your right and traffic already on the junction.

68. Q. What is a bus lane?

A. It is for the exclusive use of buses, taxis and cyclists within the specified times.

69. Q. At a road junction, where must you stop?

A. You must stop at or before the stop line.

70. Q. What should you **not** do when you are being overtaken?

A. Accelerate, or move to the right.

71. Q. What position should you adopt when turning right?

A. Just left of the centre line, except in cases of emergency.

72. Q. What is the meaning of a single continuous white line in the centre of the road?

A. It divides the road and should not be crossed except in exceptional circumstances (e.g. road traffic accident, road works etc.)

73. Q. Should you beckon pedestrians across a crossing?
   A. Never, another vehicle may be approaching.

74. Q. What sign prohibits you from entering a one way street?
   A. A round sign, white within a red circle, an arrow with a slash through it.

75. Q. What is recommended when carrying children?
   A. Child restraints and seat belts.

76. Q. What is the difference between a single yellow line and a double yellow line?
   A. On a single yellow line, parking is only permitted at certain times, on a double yellow line, parking is not permitted at all.

77. Q. What are the rules for giving arm/handsignals?
   A. Clearly and in good time, and for long enough to be understood.

78. Q. You are asked by a Garda to produce your driving licence, you don't have it with you. What is your position by law?
   A. You have 10 days to produce it at a police station of your choice. Impending legislation:— you must carry your driving licence with you for immediate production to a Garda.

79. Q. Describe motorway countdown markers?
   A. Blue with 3 bars : 300 metres; 2 bars : 200 metres; 1 bar : 100 metres.

80. Q. How long is a driving test for class B?
   A. 25 minutes approximately.

81. Q. What should you **not** do after overtaking?
   A. Cut in, or turn right or left a short distance ahead, slow down or stop.

82. Q. Name some things you should **never** do on a motorway?

A. Enter a motorway as a learner driver, exceed the speed limit, reverse, stop, walk on a motorway or cross the central reservation.

83. **Q.** When should you dip your headlights?
    A. When meeting oncoming traffic, in traffic, in built-up areas, in fog or falling snow, when following close behind another vehicle, at the beginning and end of lighting-up hours, in heavy rain and on dull days.

84. **Q.** How should you choose a good instructor?
    A. Check for qualifications i.e. DIR - MSAI - IDIA Registered. Ensure proper insurance for tuition purposes and for the D.O.E. driving test.

85. **Q.** Immediately after stopping, what control instrument should be operated first?
    A. The handbrake.

86. **Q.** When driving on country roads, what should you pay particular attention to?
    A. Persons herding animals, wandering animals, farm machinery and concealed entrances, etc.

87. **Q.** What legal requirements must you have before going to drive a vehicle?
    A. Valid licence, valid tax, valid insurance and a roadworthy vehicle.

88. **Q.** When may you drive on the right handside?
    A. In a one way street.

89. **Q.** How should you enter a roundabout?
    A. By turning left.

90. **Q.** What is the meaning of the word 'Aquaplaning'?
    A. When bald or worn tyres are unable to cope with the film of water which builds up underneath them. This leads to

a loss of control of your vehicle.

91. Q. What type of road should you never reverse into?

A. A major road. Always reverse from a major road to a minor road and also do not reverse into a one-way street or roads of equal importance.

92. Q. What colour road markings refer to the edge of a carriageway?

A. Yellow.

93. Q. Where would you expect to see a triangle painted on the road?

A. On approach to junctions, roundabouts, yield signs.

94. Q. What is the minimum age a person may start to learn to drive a car?

A. 17 years.

95. Q. What is the rule about drinking and driving?

A. You must not drink alcohol and drive.

96. Q. When about to overtake, what should you make sure of?

A. Make sure you have a clear view ahead, check mirrors to your rear, and use proper signals for long enough to be understood.

97. Q. What should you check before starting your engine?

A. That your handbrake is applied and your vehicle is in neutral gear.

98. Q. If you see double red lights flashing at a railway crossing, what would it mean to you?

A. You must not cross beyond the stop line provided. If none is provided, stop at the sign.

99. Q. What is the significance of a single white line beside a single broken line in the centre of the road?

A. You may cross if the broken white line is on your side.

Control Procedure

COCKPIT DRILL

The proper procedure should be to demonstrate to the examiner the use of the normal everyday pre-start checks:

D / S / S / S / M

Doors: Make sure all doors are properly closed.

Seats: Properly adjusted, mainly to suit your clutch control as this pedal is generally the only one that reaches the floor. Head restraints should be adjusted to your height and positioned from the nape of the neck. It is dangerous to drive without the head restraint in place or properly adjusted.

Steering: Allow the back of your seat to be sufficiently forward for your arms not to have to stretch. A proper position would be with the elbows bent.

Seat belts: Make sure you have placed your seat belts flat across your body with no twist as this could have the effect of a knife's edge in the case of a sudden stop.

Mirrors: Ensure that all available mirrors are adjusted to suit you and are kept clean at all times. Adjust inside mirror by using the top and bottom of the mirror base, without touching the glass itself.

Use of Controls

ACCELERATOR

The accelerator pedal is situated on the floor of the car, in front of the driving seat to the right. It is operated by the right foot only. As more pressure is applied, the faster the traction wheel will rotate. This is achieved by supplying the engine with more fuel. The supply of the motor fuel is controlled by the accelerator pedal through a carburettor fixed to a fuel pump. In other words, the more you press the pedal the more fuel the engine requires, the faster the vehicle will travel. If you lift the pressure from the pedal you will use less fuel and you will begin to go slower. The accelerator pedal is very sensitive to pressure and only requires gentle pressure to drive faster, or to change gear smoothly. You should be able to demonstrate your use of the accelerator smoothly and sensibly. Never accelerate too fast for the conditions you are driving in. This is for control reasons, not to mention the cost factor in doing so, as the harsher the acceleration/deceleration, the more fuel you use.

Catalytic Converters

Converters are extremely effective for the reduction of harmful levels of gases which millions of cars pour out all over the world. The catalytic converter is installed in the exhaust gas system. The exhaust system will get very hot after driving. Certain precautions should be taken. Do not park the vehicle close to easily flammable material. Never try to start the vehicle by push starting it. Always use another battery to start the vehicle. Never race or rev the engine when turning off the ignition as the catalytic converter could be damaged by unburned gas.

FOOTBRAKE

The footbrake is situated on the floor, in front of the driver, and is placed in the centre. It is operated by the right foot. When operated two red warning lights to the rear of your vehicle come on to allow following traffic know your intentions. If the speed of the vehicle you are in control of has to be reduced quickly, it will not be enough to reduce the pressure from the accelerator pedal, you must also use the footbrake. There are generally two types of brakes, disc brakes and drum brakes. Most cars have disc brakes to the front and drum brakes to the rear. Disc brakes are two pads situated behind the front wheels. When the footbrake is pressed, it squeezes the brake disc, thus reducing the rotating speed of the wheels. Drum brakes are generally fitted to the rear wheels of the vehicle, and are a set of brake shoes. When the brake is operated the shoes expand against the wheel drum from the inside, thus reducing the speed of the rotating wheels. Both types of brakes are operated by a piston in the master cylinder applying pressure to brake fluid and forwarding the fluid through a series of pipes and tubes to each individual wheel. Leaks in these tubes or pipes will result in the brakes possibly becoming ineffective or indeed failing. On most newer type cars, as a safeguard against this, there are double circuit brakes whereby two separate braking systems operate independently from each other.

The footbrake should be used with light gentle pressure at first, and then with progressively increased pressure until the required decrease in speed has been attained, or your vehicle has fully stopped. Your foot should remain on the footbrake until the handbrake has been applied. You should be able to stop smoothly and effectively without jerking.

Anti-Skid Braking System

On a vehicle without ABS (anti-skid braking system), if the brakes are applied with excessive force on a suspect road surface e.g. snow, ice, oil, wet, fallen leaves, etc. the vehicle is liable to skid. If a skid occurs the braking force will be reduced and the braking distance increased. This may lead to the driver losing control of the vehicle, with the possible consequences of the vehicle spinning out of control. With ABS the wheels are prevented from locking during braking thus maintaining the directional stability and control of the vehicle and decreasing the overall braking distance. Although the braking distance will be generally shorter with ABS, ground surface and travelling distances must be taken into consideration and the normal factors which relate to all vehicles must be adhered to as it is up to the driver to judge speed, stopping distances, cornering, etc.

Emergency Stopping

In the case of an emergency where you will have to stop quickly, you must press the brake pedal firmly without locking the wheels. Should the wheels lock then you must release your foot from the pedal and apply again quickly. This is called cadence braking where the braking is undertaken in rhythm by pumping the brake pedal. You must react quickly and brake to a controlled stop, holding the steering wheel straight and only pressing the clutch down immediately before stopping.

CLUTCH

The clutch is situated on the floor on the left hand side in front of the driver's seat. It is operated by the left foot only. The clutch consists of two discs. One disc, called a pressure plate or sometimes referred to as the fly wheel, is placed on the end of a crank axle and rotates when the engine has been engaged. The second disc is called the clutch disc (clutch plate). This is situated on an axle connected with the traction wheel through the gearbox. The clutch rotates as soon as it is pressed against the pressure plate and begins to activate as soon as the biting or gripping point is reached (a point where the two plates begin to contact), hence the power is transmitted to the wheels, via the engine, thus giving movement to your vehicle.

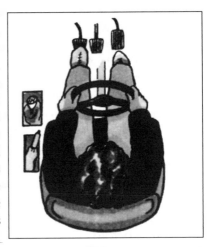

The clutch should be operated smoothly, without jerking, as this may cause the vehicle to stall. Should this happen, apply the handbrake, press the clutch pedal down, select neutral gear and restart the engine. Select first gear and lift your foot again carefully. You should be able to co-ordinate the clutch with the handbrake and accelerator. You should know and understand biting point and only use it immediately before moving away. When finished using the clutch you should remove your foot from the pedal as a partially pressed clutch will result in the burning out of the clutch. You will have to demonstrate the correct use of the co-ordination of the clutch/handbrake/ accelerator when moving away from a stationary position or from a hill.

Use of the Clutch

You should never hold your biting point for too long as it will cause a burning smell and will result in the eventual replacement of the clutch. This happens when the flywheel or ring gear (moving disc) meets the clutch disc (stationary) on the other side, and the vehicle movement is inhibited by the handbrake not being released. You will be examined with particular interest on your use of the clutch. You may misuse the clutch in many ways. If your moving away is jerky or jumpy, this may lead to a fault being marked on "use of the clutch". Other ways in which you may misuse the clutch would be coasting. You might coast in three possible ways. Firstly, you might coast to stop, i.e. pressing your clutch down or disengaging the clutch too soon before stopping. This releases the engine power from the wheels and thus frees the vehicle (possibly making it move faster initially). By maintaining and using this form of stopping, you lose the advantage of the engine power to assist the brakes in the slowing down process. Coasting in neutral is another way to misuse the clutch/gears. This means that before actually stopping your vehicle you select neutral gear and allow the vehicle to run to a stop, with or without the brakes for assistance, and thus having the same effect as the fault identified above. Thirdly, you might coast by clutching down and selecting a gear too soon, or at too high a speed, only then commencing the braking, thus travelling with your clutch down. A helpful suggestion would be these three letters B.B.C. or brakes before clutch.

GEARS

You should be able to use the gears without over revving the engine, and be able to change gears upwards or downwards before the engine labours. You must be able to maintain proper gear for the vehicle speed and road conditions. A driver should know which gear should be selected for any particular situation. In an emergency or hazard situation continue with the proper use of the gears. This is very important especially as their misuse will put your engine under considerable strain, not to mention the damage to the clutch and of course the added cost of fuel. Your examiner will note your gear selection and use, and will mark it under "Use of the Controls". Listed below is an approximate guide to gear selection for most family type cars, between 1 litre and 1.5 litres.

1st Gear = 0 - 10/15 mph (approx)
2nd Gear= 10 - 20/25 mph (approx)
3rd Gear = 20 - 30/35 mph (approx)
4th Gear = 30 - 35/40 mph (approx)
5th Gear = 40 - upwards (approx).

In most modern vehicles it may be possible to select first gear whilst the vehicle is in very slow motion. You should consult your vehicle manufacturer's handbook for gear change timings. You should not stretch your gears, i.e. do not expect or demand more of a particular gear than it was designed to deliver and do not change gear too soon. For instance, selecting fourth gear at a

speed of say 20 mph would put your engine under considerable strain and would not be very good for the clutch either. The main points an examiner looks for is what knowledge and control you have over your vehicle, e.g. what gear do you start off in, corner in, stop in, and drive in. If you must reduce your speed because of an obstruction ahead, what gear do you select to slow down in or move away again in ? Many driving instructors will advise you to step down through the gears for stops and cornering. This is not altogether necessary provided you reduce your speed sufficiently prior to your change downwards.

The generally accepted rule for the gear selection is first gear to start, second gear to corner, third gear to slow down or stop, fourth gear to drive, and fifth gear for economy drive.

Note:
If driving a lower powered vehicle, and you have been instructed to stop in second gear, then you should not now change this procedure, as this practice would not constitute a disqualification on your driving test. Some driving tutors recommend stopping in second gear especially in lower powered vehicles.

HANDBRAKE

In almost all cases, the handbrake, otherwise known as the parking brake, operates directly to the rear wheels of all vehicles, via the shoes to the inside of the wheel drum, without the assistance of brake fluid. In most cases it is situated behind the gearshift in the centre of the vehicle. It operates manually by pulling the handbrake upwards which, through a brake cable and rods, expands the shoes against the inside wheel drum, thus locking the vehicle in a stopped position. A word of caution however, you should never pull the handbrake while the vehicle is in motion as this would have a destabilising effect on your vehicle and may cause a skid as in most cars the handbrake only operates on the rear wheels. However, you may use it in an emergency in the unlikely event of total brake failure.

You should use the handbrake only when required. Never pull it up on the ratchet as this will put undue wear and tear on the locking/holding mechanism. Always use the Press-Pull-Release procedure to engage. To release use the Lift-Press-Return to regain to the normal disengaged position. On most modern vehicles a warning (red) light shows on the dash board controls to show that the handbrake is engaged. Always ensure that this warning light is extinguished whilst driving.

STEERING

The correct way to hold the steering wheel is to have your hands in the Ten to Two or Quarter to Three positions. You operate the steering controls by rotating the steering wheel through the pull-push method. This movement, either to the left or right, will cause connecting joints to turn the front wheels. You should always maintain control of the steering by keeping both hands on the steering wheel, except when operating a signal or a vehicle control. After turning the steering wheel, say for a left or right corner, the steering wheel will want to straighten automatically. This is called self-centring. This happens when you allow the steering wheel to slip through your hands. This practice is not recommended, as the self-centring or straightening up will occur at different speeds depending on your travelling speed. You should always return the steering wheel by using the push-pull method.

CORRECT METHOD OF STEERING

Normal holding + driving position		Recommended holding position ten to two or a quarter to three
Slide left hand to top (12 o'clock)		Right hand holding wheel
Left hand (gripping lightly) pulls down wheel (6 o'clock)		Right hand slides down (6 o'clock)
Slide left hand to top again (12 o'clock)		Right hand pushes up (12 o'clock)
Left hand pulls down (6 o'clock)		Right hand slides down again (6 o'clock)

You would be marked down on the use of steering for any of the following bad habits: crossing of the hands/arms in either turning left or right; resting the right arm on the window or arm rest (whilst driving) or resting your hand on your lap or knee, or rimming the wheel, i.e. placing your hand on the inside of the steering wheel to turn.

Power Steering
Most new vehicles manufactured today have what is known as P.A.S. or power assisted steering. P.A.S. is operated through the engine via power fluid which makes the steering feel very light to the touch and very easy to turn. Time must be taken to get used to his "feel". Coming from a vehicle without power steering, which takes more manual effort, there are some possible dangers for the first time user of P.A.S. Because of the effortless manoeuvring of the steering wheel, you may just get into the corner too soon, and possibly mount the kerb on a left hand corner. When the engine is stopped the power steering will not function and will require more manual effort to operate. You should note this fact when being towed without the assistance of the engine. It is also inadvisable to switch off your engine while moving.

HORN
A suitable one tone horn must be fitted to all vehicles to give suitable audible warning of approach, if and when necessary. It is illegal to fit a bell, gong, siren, or a two tone instrument to your vehicle. When a motor vehicle is stationary on a road, no person shall use or permit to use any warning instrument (except for safety reasons). However, public service vehicles, large or small, are allowed to fit an audible warning for summoning assistance in the case of theft, attempted theft, personal attack or injury. Many people are reluctant to use the

horn on a driving test when in fact at times it is imperative. For instance, it could be used to gain the attention of a pedestrian who is about to step on to the road in front of you, and who you do not think is aware of your presence. Another instance is where there is a sharp turn where visibility is limited or obscured. Normal use of the horn should not be aggressive or excessive. The use of the horn is not allowed between the hours of 23.30 and 07.00, except for traffic reasons or in an emergency.

SIGNALS

The correct use of signals is of the utmost importance. You should signal clearly and in good time before moving from the normal driving position, before changing position to turn, before changing lanes, slowing down or stopping, etc. In fact, always give a signal if it will be of benefit to another road user. Most vehicles have the operational signal control attached to the steering column, to the right or the left. The simple rule to remember is that the directional arm will always follow the direction of the steering wheel. There is a self-cancelling mechanism for most turns past the twelve o'clock position on the steering wheel, however, for gentle changes of direction, and indeed some roundabouts, this will not self-cancel and must be done manually. Hand/arm signals are also very important and you will be expected to demonstrate your knowledge of them. (See pages 73 and 74 for hand/arm signals.) Another form of signalling to other drivers is the brake lights positioned to the rear of the vehicle.

Whatever form of signal you are using, you must not over signal or give a misleading signal.

MIRRORS

Legally, all motor vehicles in category B must have rear view mirrors fitted. The interior mirror is the main mirror and is strategically placed in the centre of the vehicle to give the best view to the rear. It should be adjusted by holding the top and bottom frame so as not to smudge the glass as a thumb print will reflect and distort your vision, especially at night. It should be adjusted to take in the four corners of the rear window. Mirrors should be checked regularly along the way to understand what is happening behind and to the rear and sides of your vehicle.

Check mirrors before making any type of manoeuvre from the straight position, e.g. moving out for any obstruction along your intended path, for overtaking a stationary vehicle, bicycle, motorbike, or roadworks, etc. You should always check your mirrors before using the signals and before accelerating or de-accelerating.

Overtaking Mirrors

Door mirrors on vehicles are a legal obligation. Mirrors have blindspots (see Blindspot section) so it is imperative that you do not rely entirely on them before moving away or overtaking. All new cars must have driver and passenger door mirrors fitted, otherwise known as "overtaking mirrors". These mirrors should be adjusted to suit the driver's vision and should give the best possible view from behind and to the sides of your vehicle, but not too much of the vehicle side body.

You must always look over your shoulder/s when about to move away from a stationary position. Overtaking mirrors are convex mirrors, which basically means that whatever you view through them will be smaller and further away than they really are. Convex mirrors are designed to take in a wider view of the rear sides of your vehicle. The interior mirror is the one that will give you the true size of vehicle and distance from behind.

BLINDSPOTS

Before moving away you must look over your shoulders. There are at least six blindspots in a vehicle. These blindspots are a minimum of 67 feet to the rear of your vehicle on both sides. On the average road your blindspot is over the length of two buses.

All cars have blindspots, but there can be a major difference between the types of vehicles, and their blindspot areas. Ask your driving instructor to demonstrate this area. These do not just occur at the points shown in the diagram i.e. behind the framework of the vehicle. It is everything behind your left and right ears. The door mirrors will take in some of this area, but they will not cover the full blindspot area. A good test of where blindspots are may be checked by pulling in somewhere safe and 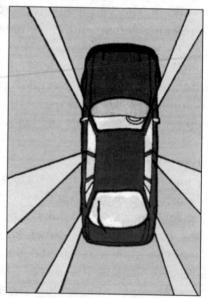 convenient on the left. Watch a particular road user approach. As they pass your shoulder, wait until you see them come into view in your centre mirror. Immediately then you may look around to see just how far they have travelled, that is your blindspot area, i.e. the area covered by that particular road user from the time they went out of view. This area of blindspot travels with you as you drive.

Failing to undertake full observation will result in you failing your test.

OVERTAKING

Sometimes it is necessary to overtake moving vehicles whilst driving, even on your driving test. Most candidates are reluctant to do this as any of their overtaking exercises would most likely have been of stationary vehicles, or vehicles slowing down to stop a short distance ahead. The dangers associated with this exercise concern speed and location.

You must train yourself to read the road ahead, and assess every road and traffic situation before making the decision to overtake. The importance of full concentration and anticipation whilst driving or overtaking cannot be over-stressed as overtaking is possibly one of the most dangerous activities for the part experienced driver. Firstly, you must decide if it is really necessary to overtake. Once this decision is made, you must now check the road from behind and in front of you. You must signal right your intention to following traffic and those on-coming. You must assess the speed and length of the vehicle to be overtaken. You must never overtake unless you are sure you can complete the exercise without being a hindrance or danger to any other road user. Once you have started to overtake, move briskly past the vehicle you are overtaking, and leave plenty of room. Only when you have the full view of the vehicle in your rear view mirror, may you move back in fully. It is not totally necessary to signal left to return to the normal driving position. When overtaking motorcyclists, cyclists, horse and riders, or any other animals you must allow plenty of room. You must only overtake on the right, with the following exceptions:

1. when a driver in front has signalled their intention to turn right, and you have space on the left, without being in the way of others
2. when you wish to turn left at a controlled junction with a filter arrow to the left
3. when traffic is moving slower in traffic queues on the right hand lane
4. in one way streets, where traffic may pass on either side. (dual carriageways are not one way streets).

You should take extra care when overtaking in conditions of poor visibility and at night when it is more difficult to judge speed and distance of other vehicles.

Common Mistakes in Overtaking

1. indecision while holding an outside position
2. failing to observe correctly
3. not overtaking when it would have been safe to do so
4. getting too close to a vehicle in front before overtaking
5. too close to a junction, bridge, corner or bend
6. close to a hump back bridge or brow of a hill
7. where the road ahead narrows
8. on the approach to a pedestrian crossing or any other crossing of solid white lines
9. driving over any diagonal stripes or chevrons where it would make another road user change speed or direction.

If at any time during your test you cause another road user to change speed or direction you will fail your test.

POSITION ON THE ROAD

Always maintain the correct position on the road to the left, as close as practicable to the kerb. Always give a safe clearance to cyclists and pedestrians and, when overtaking parked vehicles expect the unexpected. Follow the correct course on turning right and left and be particularly careful on position at approach to roundabouts. Always pay attention to the rear and sides of your vehicle for motorbikes and cyclists. When in your position, whilst following other traffic, with no intention of overtaking, you should maintain your distance from the vehicle in front by at least one metre for every mile of your speed in normal traffic. This may not be possible within built up areas. On faster type roads a longer distance of at least 10 times the quoted distance would be advised, and especially in fog or falling snow, or any other adverse weather conditions.

Procedure on Turning Right

This is one of the most common areas for mistakes for learners on test. Mistakes are made mainly on the approach procedure and positioning of the vehicle. Well before you intend to turn you must check your mirrors to have a clear picture of the following traffic, which is more important in turning right than left as you will also be changing position on the road. The correct procedure is mirror, signal, mirror, position, speed, look. Check mirror first to ensure that the following traffic is not too close. Signal and check that enough time and distance have been given to the following traffic to understand and act upon your signals. Begin to move to a left-of-centre position on the road and maintain this position and signal until you have a clear road ahead. Proceed only when you have a clear road by turning right and maintaining a view of your rear mirror for the following traffic situation. While waiting to turn right your steering wheels should never be turned to the right because if you were rear ended by a following vehicle you would be pushed forward into the oncoming traffic.

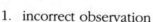

Common Areas for Mistakes in Turning Right

The most common areas for examiners marking candidates on right turns are:

1. incorrect observation
2. waiting unduly for oncoming traffic
3. proceeding when it is not safe to do so
4. cutting of right hand corners
5. failing to look into the road in which you wish to travel
6. failing to adopt and maintain the correct position after the turn is completed on the new road
7. over-steering, thus leading to incorrect position
8. moving out without proper observation
9. waiting to turn right in the wrong holding position
10. failing to take possession of the junction when it would be safe and correct to do so
11. not understanding filter traffic lights.

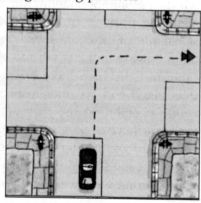

Other areas where learners are slow to proceed would be at traffic light controlled junctions, or decision in undertaking the turning nearside to nearside (passenger to passenger) or offside to offside (driverside to driverside).

The general rule of offside to offside is acceptable, nearside to nearside is preferable, but both are legal. The general rule when turning right at traffic light controlled junctions is never to be the third car in a junction unless it can accommodate your vehicle without hindering an oncoming vehicle wishing to turn right.

When wishing to turn right from a dual carriageway, the same procedure should be undertaken but you will be changing lanes to the right hand lane.

Yellow Box Junctions
You should never enter and wait in a yellow box junction unless your exit road is clear. One exception to this rule is that you can enter and wait in a yellow box if you are turning right and your exit road is clear.

Procedure on Turning Left

Before any type of manoeuvre or slowing down, you will need to know the following traffic position, to assess the speeds of following vehicles, and realise that your actions will affect others. You slowing down will generally mean that others will have to do the same. So it is imperative that the same procedure is followed as for right hand turns, i.e. mirror, signal, mirror, followed by position, speed and look. Firstly, you should check your mirror to assess the following traffic. Signal your intention to turn left, again check the following traffic and begin to reduce your speed. Position your vehicle close to the left for the imminent left hand turn, and look into the junction in which you are going to travel. After completing the manoeuvre, you should always check your mirrors for the new road for the following traffic. If you are driving a long vehicle or articulated vehicle you may need to move to the right before commencing the turning. Watch for overtaking traffic in your mirrors, also paying particular attention for any traffic coming up on the inside (left) e.g. cyclists and motorcyclists.

Common Areas for Mistakes in Turning Left

Some of the most common areas for mistakes are:
1. speed on the approach to a left hand turn
2. selecting the wrong gear for the corner
3. holding an outside position when signalling to turn left
4. moving right (while signalling left) just before the turn
5. incorrect observation
6. proceeding when it is not safe to do so
7. failing to look into the road in which you intend travel
8. failing to maintain the correct position after the turn is completed on the new road

9. over or under steering, thus leading to incorrect position
10. moving out without proper observation
11. not understanding filter traffic lights.

DRIVING AN AUTOMATIC TRANSMISSION VEHICLE

The term "automatic" means that a vehicle with a gear ratio between the engine and the wheels can only be varied by the use of the accelerator or the brakes. Finding a driving school with an automatic transmission tuition vehicle may be difficult. However, you will find that if you have the use of an automatic transmission vehicle at your disposal, and that you are insured to drive it, most instructors will give lessons in your car. When you undertake and pass a driving test in an automatic vehicle, you will be given a certificate of competence with the words "Limited to vehicles with automatic transmission".

In all automatic vehicles, there are generally only two foot pedals, an accelerator and a brake. These will be operated by the right foot. There is a gear selector in place of a gear shift. The typical selector has the following gear positions:

P = Park   **D** = Drive
R = Reverse   **2** = Second Gear
N = Neutral   **1** = First Gear

Driving an automatic vehicle is fundamentally different from a manual gear change vehicle as all the controls are operated by the right foot. The left foot is redundant. You must train your left foot to do absolutely nothing.

D: when the "D" is selected the gears will change automatically. This is governed by the pressure applied to the accelerator pedal (see Accelerator section). This gear change is commonly known as kick down and takes into account the road conditions and the load the vehicle has to carry. The gear box will automatically change downward if the vehicle is travelling uphill and a lower gear is required. Another example would be that should you begin to slow down, and then wish to move away again, then the gear will automatically adjust to the correct gear suitable for that speed.

1 and 2: These are known as the lock-up positions. On an automatic vehicle (see diagram) you may desire to hold a position in 1st or 2nd gear. Choosing 2nd, the gear change will still make automatic gear changes, but only as high as 2nd. Lock-up prevents an untimely gear change when overtaking, or on an icy uphill movement, or a steep descent, where the engine resistance would or could be desirable. However, you should not select a lock-up position to slow you down.

P: When the Park position is selected the transmission is in neutral and the vehicle is locked mechanically against any movement. This position should always be selected whenever you park your vehicle and, along with the handbrake, it will hold the car in position. You may also start the vehicle in this position. Never select "P" while the vehicle is moving as this could damage the vehicle's transmission.

N: The Neutral position enables the vehicle to remain in neutral. You may also start the vehicle in this mode.

When stopped at traffic lights the normal routine is to leave the transmission in gear or in the "D" position for short stops. However, always maintain your footbrake. In traffic and especially for an uphill start also use your handbrake. For longer periods, the handbrake should be applied and the gear selector should be returned to the neutral position. You may then release your foot from the brake pedal, as the glare of the brake lights, especially on a wet or dark night may dazzle the following driver.

THE USE OF GEARS IN AN AUTOMATIC CAR

Driving: After starting the engine with the selector lever in the "N" (Neutral) or the "P" (Park) position, select the range desired and depress the accelerator.

"P" *(Park)*: This position is to be used with the parking brake. It must never be used when the vehicle is in motion. "P" is one of only 2 positions (the other is "N") in which your vehicle may be started.

"R" *(Reverse)*: For backing up / reversing: bring the vehicle to a complete stop before shifting into this range.

"N" *(Neutral)*: This position must be used when the vehicle is towed and can be used when starting the engine.

"D" *(Drive):* This position is for all normal forward driving. If more speed is needed for overtaking, press the accelerator pedal hard to the floor. This will give you the acceleration you need at once.

"2" *(Second):* You may choose this position when going down a moderate gradient (hill) where you want to slow down a little without using the brakes. Shift back into the "D" position to return to normal driving.

"1" *(Low):* Use this position when strong retardation effect is needed on a steep descent. Shift back to "D" (Drive) range so that the vehicle will again upshift into direct drive.

WHERE STATED CORRECTIVE LENSES MUST ALWAYS BE WORN

TRAFFIC LIGHTS AND SYSTEMS

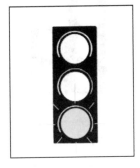

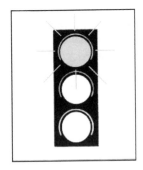

Green
You may proceed if the way ahead is clear.

Amber
Stop at the stop line. You may only go on if the amber appears after you have crossed the stop line or are so close to it that to stop might cause an accident.

Red
Stop. Wait behind the stop line.

If movement is allowed only in one direction, a green arrow pointing in that direction may replace the full green. Signs are often used with these signals to indicate the necessary movement or to prohibit turns.

IN THE ABSENCE OF ANY SIGNS, ALWAYS ASSUME 30 MPH

When this green arrow is displayed as well as a full green signal you may turn right while opposite traffic is held at a red signal. At the same time the full green signal allows the movement of traffic in other directions.

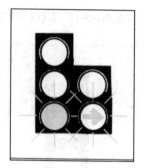

Traffic may proceed straight ahead or turn left. No right turn allowed.

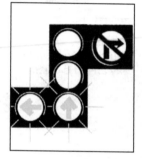

A green arrow may be provided in addition to the full green signal if movement in a certain direction is allowed before or after the full green phase. If the way is clear you may go, but only in the direction shown by the arrow.

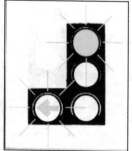

TAKE EFFECTIVE OBSERVATION AT ALL JUNCTIONS

Examples of road traffic light systems

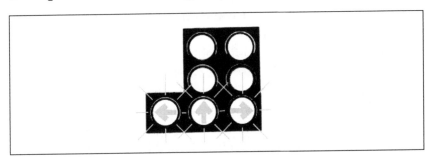

You may proceed, right / left / straight

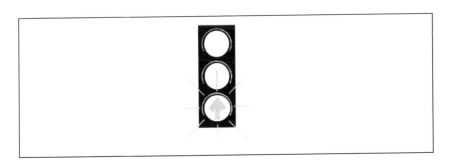

You may proceed in direction of arrow only, (straight ahead)

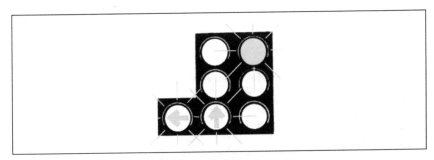

You may only proceed left/straight and must wait for an arrow to turn right

Understanding Filter Lights

Probably one of the most common areas for candidates to be marked for lack of progress is at controlled junctions either on turning right or left at filter traffic lights.

Assuming a traffic light situation where you wish to turn right at a filter light or arrow, a filter light may operate after the full green phase. The tendency for some candidates is to hold back behind the stop line on a full green light waiting for the right arrow to operate. A major point to remember about this particular situation is that if a full green light is on with no visible red light, you should treat this junction as a normal green light procedure: Proceed with caution, placing the front of your car in line with the centre line of the road onto which you wish to turn. Wait for all oncoming vehicles to pass and then proceed as normal.

The only time you would have to stop is if there were green directional arrows pointing straight and left and a red light against you for turning right. In this situation you must stop behind the stop line and wait for a full green light or arrow in your favour.

Green arrows

When a green arrow lights beside a green light this is to advise you that traffic coming through from the opposite direction has been stopped by a red light and you may safely turn right provided junction is clear.

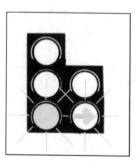

TREAT BROKEN TRAFFIC LIGHTS AS STOP SIGNS

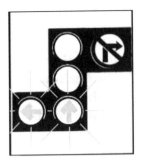

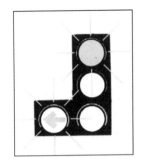

Traffic may proceed straight ahead or turn left - no right turn allowed.

Traffic may proceed straight ahead only.

Traffic may turn left even though other traffic is halted by red light.

Pedestrian lights (rules for drivers)

Stop and wait behind stop line.

Stop, unless the vehicle is so close to the stop line that it cannot be halted safely before crossing the stop line.

Flashing Amber Light Yield to pedestrians but proceed with caution if crossing is clear.

Zig Zag markings may also be provided at pedestrian lights. Where they are provided, the rules are simple, no stopping other than for traffic reasons.

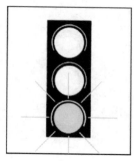

Proceed if way is clear

Note: Remember the flashing amber light allows you to proceed only if the crossing is clear - watch out for pedestrians who might step out suddenly.

TURNABOUT

On the day of your driving test, you will be required to demonstrate a turnabout. This manoeuvre is commonly called a three point turn, however, it does not necessarily have to be completed in three movements. The main reason for this exercise is to demonstrate to the examiner that you have a reasonable standard and proficiency in the control and use of your vehicle. The examiner will also take note of your general observation vis-à-vis pedestrian traffic etc. before and during the manoeuvre. How you check your blind spots, especially at points A, B, C and D will also be noted (see diagram page 48).

Points to remember
   a. general observation including blind spots
   b. the full and proper use of steering
   c. use of feet and hand controls

1. Put a full right hand lock as you start, driving slowly across the road in first gear. Approximately 2 to 3 feet from the far kerb, change the steering to a full left hand lock. Brake before the front wheels touch the kerb.

2. Apply reverse gear and reverse slowly towards the opposite kerb. This will have the effect of the back of your vehicle moving left and the front of the vehicle moving right in preparation for the next movement. Again, 2 to 3 feet from the opposite kerb, turn your steering wheel to the right and brake before the rear wheels touch the kerb.

3. You may now apply first gear and move away slowly. Generally you would pull in on the left and wait for further instructions from your examiner.

Note: You may not be able to complete this manoeuvre in three movements due to the size of the vehicle, the width of the road, your overall skill in handling the vehicle or some obstruction along your intended path of the manoeuvre.

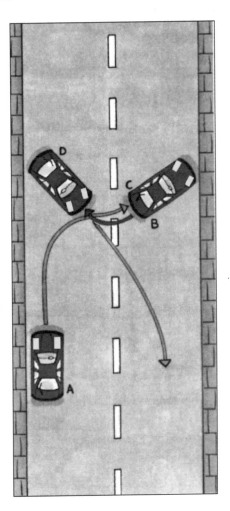

Use of Steering during Turnabout

The general pull-push movement of the steering does not have to be rigidly applied here. However, you may not steer while the vehicle is stopped. The steering should be used briskly at a controlled forward/reverse speed.

Use of Signals

It is not necessary to use any signals during the turnabout manoeuvre.

Use of Handbrake during Turnabout

The use of the handbrake is recommended but is not obligatory. For instance, you may wish to use it everytime you stop (see diagram at points A, B, C and D) especially if you feel a camber (slope towards the side of the road), which will make you use it. Whichever way you decide or are familiar with, you should maintain a certain progression throughout the whole exercise.

Note: To begin this manoeuvre, pull in on the left somewhere safe and convenient. Always ensure you do not cause an obstruction when you stop. Always ensure good visibility before you start and choose a place where you can complete the manoeuvre without driving or reversing into any obstruction along the road, e.g. a kerbside pole or a tree.

HILL STARTS

During the course of a driving test, you will be expected to demonstrate a hill start. Your examiner will ask you in words such as these:

"Somewhere safe and convenient, I would like you to pull in on the left, please."

This means that you must check your mirror and signal your intention to pull in, always making sure you don't infringe on the rights of others, paying special attention to pedestrians and cyclists. After stopping, you should:

1. apply the handbrake
2. select neutral
3. cancel your signals

Note: Never stop your car on the handbrake. Your car should be stopped fully on the footbrake and then your handbrake applied.

Also cancel signals. It is all too easy to hear the indicators 'clicking' and to assume that you are using the proper signal to move away again.

Moving Away On a Hill

Remember this manoeuvre is much the same as moving away from any stationary position: **P** (= prepare) **O** (= observe) **M** (= move).

'**P**' To prepare your car for imminent move off, you must first press your clutch down (depress) and select 1st gear. Increase the revs of the engine to create more power for the vehicle to leave. Allow your clutch up slowly until you find the 'biting point', and hold that position, that is to say, when you feel the car almost ready to move.

NB: Never hold this position for too long a period as this would result in you burning out your clutch.

'**O**' Observe. This entails checking around the vehicle and using your mirrors and when you have a clear road from behind, check your blindspots (see page 48). You may now signal your intention to move away.

NB: Never use the overtaking mirror only (driver's door mirror) for this manoeuvre as it will not give you a true view of what is behind. Remember your centre mirror is the one you will be mainly marked on (except in vehicles with limited visibility, where the full use of external mirrors would be essential).

'**M**' To move away from this position, you may now increase the amount of gas (accelerator) as the clutch coordinates with the release of the handbrake, continually checking your mirrors as you leave. You may have to cancel the signal manually, as the cancellation mechanism will normally only work on almost a full turn of the steering wheel.

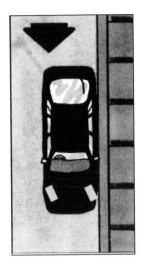  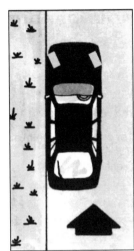

Parking On a Hill

When you park downhill and are leaving your car, turn your steering wheel into the kerb or towards the side of the road and apply the handbrake. Leave the car in reverse gear.

When you park uphill, turn your steering wheel away from the kerb and let your vehicle roll back a few inches until the rear of one front wheel gently touches the kerb. Then apply the parking brake. Leave the car in first gear.

If there is no kerb turn the wheels towards the side of the road so the car will roll away from the centre of the road if the brakes fail and your car is not left in gear.

When you park on a sloping driveway, turn the wheels so that the car will not roll into the street if the brakes fail.

Always apply your handbrake and leave the vehicle in gear. If your vehicle has an automatic transmission, always use the park position.

ROUNDABOUTS

On approach to a roundabout you must give way to those already on it. You enter by turning left, giving way to traffic on your right. The correct use of signals is very important for the ease and free movement of traffic on roundabouts.

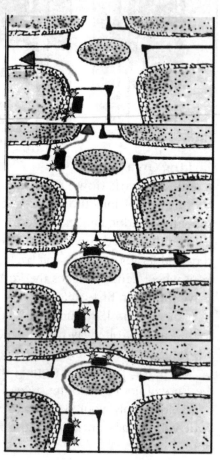

1st exit (assuming a left corner)
Position: left
Signal: left

2nd exit
Position: left
Signal: left after you pass the first exit

3rd exit or more
Position: right (left of centre)
Signal: right on approach and maintain this signal until you reach the exit before the one you wish to take. You then change to lefthand signal to leave. Check mirror and change position to left and leave roundabout.
Note: Some roundabouts have only 3 exits. However, the best way to approach this type of roundabout is: any turn past 12 o'clock on a clock face, signal right followed by a left. E.g.: position here of 2nd exit is in the place of 3rd exit above and should be treated the same.

REVERSE CORNER
(A limited opening to the left)

Main points: A. Observation
                   B. Manoeuvrability
                   C. Control

1. Before you begin to reverse, look around fully to make certain that no children are near the rear of your vehicle. Then check your blindspots. When in reverse, always look through the rear of your vehicle except in vans, trucks etc., where visibility is limited.
2. Reverse slowly maintaining progress straight back until your rear wheels are in line with the start of the corner.
3. When your wheels are level start turning into your corner, pulling left for left corner, right for right corner, looking around for nearby traffic.
4. As your vehicle rounds the corner, it will help if you look at the kerbside far ahead as you come round.
5. As soon as your rear wheels come close to the kerb, you may straighten the wheels, checking around for oncoming traffic, children etc.
6. Throughout this manoeuvre you will be required to have full observation and control of your vehicle.

Note:

Never reverse into a one-way street.

Never reverse from a minor road onto a major road.

USE OF HAND/ARM SIGNALS

On the day of your driving test, you will be expected to demonstrate the use of hand/arm signals. This usually takes place after you reverse around a corner (limited opening to the left). The words the examiner generally uses would be: "In the absence of mechanical signals (indicators), I would like you to demonstrate how you would show a pointsman that you wish to go left/right, etc."

There are three signals for a pointsman and three for traffic behind you; two 'in car' and four 'out of car'.

Let us begin with a pointsman. A pointsman is a garda on point duty. You might expect to see one where traffic lights are not working, or at a racetrack entrance or event where lights would not normally be needed.

Question

How would you show:

1. a pointsman that you are going left?
2. a pointsman that you are going straight?
3. a pointsman that you are going right?
4. traffic behind that you are going right?
5. traffic behind that you are going left?
6. traffic behind that you are slowing down or stopping?

Answers

A.1. Your right opened hand and forearm pointed to the left, high enough and for long enough over the dashboard for it to be seen.

A.2. Your left opened hand (palm forward) under your centre mirror pointed forward.

A.3. Right hand/arm out of window, palm forward, pointing right.

A.4. Right hand/arm out of window, palm forward, pointing right.

A.5. Open hand/arm out of window and move hand and arm in an anticlockwise direction.

A.6. Open hand/arm out of window, palm downwards, up and down movement.

Note: All signals, mechanical or otherwise, must be given clearly and decisively and for long enough to be understood.

Motorways

Motorways are now becoming part of the Irish way of life, but as in all other countries, learner drivers are not permitted to use them.

Special regulations apply to motorways, these include:
- no learner drivers
- no invalid carriages
- no pedal cyclists
- no motorcycles under 50cc (cylinder capacity)
- no pedestrians
- no animals
- no reversing
- no U-turns
- no vehicle, large or small, not capable of reaching a maximum speed of 30 mph
- no stopping

Note: Because of restricted parking areas on motorways, never attempt to enter a motorway on low fuel, always check tyre pressure and that all legal requirements on your vehicle are met.

Speed

Motorways are different from any other types of roads as they are designed to cater for a large volume of traffic travelling at high speeds. Most accidents on motorways occur during overtaking but other major considerations must be taken into account. These are:

- the state of your health
- the state and condition of your vehicle
- under or over-estimation of your own speed, or the speed of others
- travelling distances between you and other vehicles
- distance between you and the vehicle you wish to overtake
- under-estimation of the wind strength (crosswinds) because of the open areas on motorways
- the road construction, i.e. road width, road size, ascents and descents and road curves.

Learners are not allowed to use motorways, however the rules for motorways should be learned as questions about them will be asked in the theory test. After passing your test it is advisable to have motorway driving lessons.

Fog

Fog on motorways can be a killer because of the vast open spaces. You should always drive on headlights and/or front and rear fog lamps. Keep your distance and remember, don't play 'Follow the leader'. Many cars and trucks have left the motorway over the central reserve to meet oncoming traffic on the other side by simply following the rear lights of the car in front.

Remember – Keep your distance.

Signs for motorways

These are blue with a white border and give information for place distances, route numbers and lanes. Because of the high speed attained by some drivers, things happen very fast, so it is advisable to plan your route. Take note of your destination and the exit number, which is normally located on the bottom left corner of an early information sign. These signs would normally be in advance of one mile from your turning, written in white on a blue background. Be especially alert whilst driving on motorways, as full concentration is required at all times.

Remember the maximum speed limits for heavy goods vehicles, buses and coaches. (See current *Rules of the Road*).

The following are some signs you will encounter on the motorway:

Motorway signs

The start of a motorway

Direction sign at the commencement of a motorway. The M number and blue background indicate that this is a motorway route: the motorway symbol indicates that motorway regulations will apply immediately.

Distance markers indicate the distance to the start of the deceleration lane – each bar represents 100 metres.

On motorways early information is given about junctions.

The first sign is usually located one mile in advance: it gives the number of the road leading from the junction and, in a black panel, the number of the junction.

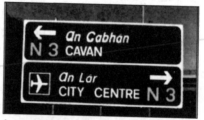

A route direction sign is usually located at the separation of the deceleration lane from the main carriageway.

The third sign, at the beginning of the deceleration lane, also adds the principal destinations ahead.

The next sign, usually at half a mile, adds the main traffic destination which can be reached by leaving the motorway.

End of motorway

Failing The Test and The Fail Form

TOP TWELVE REASONS FOR FAILING A TEST

Listed below are the most common reasons for failing a driving test, not necessarily in order of frequency:

1. lack of control in moving off
2. failing to yield right of way as required
3. not looking in your mirrors correctly and regularly
4. not making reasonable progress along the road
5. failing to reduce speed on approach to a junction
6. failing to look left as necessary at road junctions turning left
7. failing to act and comply with road signs
8. incorrect position and procedure when turning right
9. overtaking incorrectly
10. incorrect road position and lack of lane discipline
11. misuse of clutch, i.e. coasting
12. lack of control and observation in reverse manoeuvre

All of the above are serious flaws in your driving and would result in you being refused a certificate of competency. You would then have to re-apply for another test and wait the required period of time for another appointment. Your driver tester is not permitted to discuss the driving test with you. If, however, you feel you do not agree with the ruling, you may write to the supervisor in charge: Driver Testing Section, Government Buildings, Ballina, Co. Mayo. Tel: 096-70677

Failing this, you would have to appeal to the district court which would rule on your case and give a final decision.

You may be granted a re-test. However, this may be done by a driver tester with a supervisor in the back of the car or by the supervisor himself. A supervisor may sit in on any test being conducted. This will not affect your driving test or your examiner's overall decision to pass or fail you. The main reason for this is to have uniformity among all driver testers. This assists the Department in monitoring faults and markings in which the examiners were trained.

REFUSAL OF APPLICATION FOR A CERTIFICATE OF COMPETENCY

This form is given to candidates who fail the driving test (all categories). It details the faults accrued during the driving test, and is sectioned into subsections. These sections make it easy for you to understand the faults which made you unsuccessful (see sample fail/refusal sheet).

The main sections are:
- Road and Lane Position
- Overtaking/Passing
- Anticipation/Observation
- Mirror/s – Signals
- Right of Way
- Progress
- Speed
- Traffic Controls

- Vehicle Controls
- Reverse
- Turnabout
- Parking
- Courtesy
- Motorcyclists

DEPARTMENT OF THE ENVIRONMENT

DRIVING TEST REPORT

NAME: _____   DATE: _____

The items on which faults occurred during the driving test are marked below. The faults are graded as follows:-
X Serious Fault; ❑ More than one serious fault repeated; **O** Disqualifying (dangerous or potentially dangerous) fault.
In preparing for another test you should pay particular attention to the items marked below. Further information on these and other aspects of the test are contained in the booklet entitled "Rules of The Road" which is available at Post Offices and the leaflet "The Driving Test" (copy herewith).

1. **RULES OF THE ROAD**
   - You must have a satisfactory knowledge of the Rules of the Road.
2. **ROAD AND LANE POSITION**
   - In normal driving maintain correct position on the straight/on bends/within traffic lanes.
   - Keep a safe distance from the vehicle in front.
   - Follow correct course at cross-junctions/ roundabouts
   - Follow correct course turning right/ turning right from one-way streets
   - Follow correct course turning left
   - On stopping be in a safe position and do not cause obstruction. Do not bump/mount kerb.
3. **OVERTAKING/PASSING**
   - Allow sufficient but not excessive clearance to pedestrians/cyclists/stationary vehicles/other traffic/other objects
   - Do not overtake when it is dangerous or prohibited to do so.
4. **ANTICIPATION/OBSERVATION**
   - Take proper observation when moving off/changing lanes/overtaking/turning right/turning left/at roundabouts/at cross-junctions
   - React correctly to hazards.
   - Anticipate what others may do.
5. **MIRRORS**
   - Use mirror(s) properly and in good time before signalling/moving off/on the straight/overtaking/ changing lane/at roundabouts/ turning right/ turning left/slowing/stopping.
6. **SIGNALS**
   - Give correct signal in good time before moving off/overtaking/changing lane/at roundabouts/ turning right/turning left/slowing/stopping.
   - Cancel signal after use.
   - Demonstrate hand-signals correctly.
   - Do not beckon pedestrians/other road users on the road.
7. **RIGHT OF WAY**
   - Yield right of way as required moving off/ overtaking/changing lane/at junctions/at roundabouts/turning right/turning left.

8. **SPEED**
   - Adjust speed to suit traffic and road conditions/on approach to junctions/roundabouts/traffic controls/ when turning right/when turning left.
9. **PROGRESS**
   - Maintain reasonable progress moving off/on the straight/overtaking/at junctions/at roundabouts/ turning left/turning right/avoid causing obstruction.
   - Maintain reasonable progress turning left/turning right at traffic lights. Avoid causing obstruction.
10. **TRAFFIC CONTROLS**
    - Comply with traffic lights/road signs/road markings/pedestrian crossings and signals given by Gardai/school wardens/persons in charge of animals.
11. **VEHICLE CONTROLS**
    - Make proper use of accelerator/clutch/gears/ footbrake/handbrake/ steering. Do not coast. Do not roll back.
12. **REVERSE**
    - Manoeuvre competently, with adequate observation and consideration for other road users.
13. **TURNABOUT**
    - Manoeuvre competently, with adequate observation and consideration for other road users.
14. **PARK**
    - Park correctly/legally.
15. **COURTESY**
    - Show due regard for the safety and convenience of other road users.
16. **MOTORCYCLISTS**
    - Look around before moving off/overtaking/ changing lane/turning right/turning left/stopping and at roundabouts.
    - Give correct hand signals in good time.
    - Keep motorcycle under control while signalling and complete signal before making turn to ensure that both hands will be on handlebars when turning.
    - Perform 'U' turn correctly, taking proper observation.
    - Maintain proper control of motorcycle at slow speed.
    - Steer a correct course.

But let us move on to the form itself. The markings for these faults are coded as follows:

- An '**X**' is for a serious fault. This is where a proper procedure was not followed or undertaken.
- A box '❑'is for more than one serious fault or this fault repeated.
- A circle '**O**' symbolises the main reason why you have failed your test. A disqualifying fault or a pattern of serious faults will bring about the failure of your driving test.

You will also be given a 4 page document, *"The Driving Test"*, which details what an examiner would expect you to do on a test. Its initial purpose is to explain your faults, along with the Fail form.

The general idea of the Fail Form is to help you identify your mistakes and have your faults corrected before returning to do another test. If you are only now going to a driving school, you should bring this form to your instructor who will then be able to check and identify these faults in your driving to see if they are still present. In any case this form should not be destroyed as you will need it to gain a third or subsequent provisional licence from the relevant licensing authority. After a refusal of a Certificate of Competency, the normal waiting period before re-sitting your test is 4 weeks from the previous test date. However, certain discretions may be made in urgent cases by writing or contacting the supervisor in charge and asking to be put on a cancellation list at a test centre of your choice.

Test Yourself

Typical Format and Layout of the Theory Test
(Answers on page 91)

1. What is the overall stopping distance at 30mph?
- ☐ a. 20 ft or 6 metres
- ☐ b. 80 ft or 24 metres
- ☐ c. 75 ft or 23 metres

2. On dull days should you drive on:
- ☐ a. main beam
- ☐ b. dipped head lights
- ☐ c. side lights

3. What are rear fog lights for?
- ☐ a. night driving
- ☐ b. rain
- ☐ c. conditions of poor visibility only

4. What does a flash from an oncoming car mean?
- ☐ a. you may go
- ☐ b. have a nice day
- ☐ c. beware of my presence

5. Why are yellow boxes used on junctions?
- ☐ a. job creation for painters
- ☐ b. to keep junctions free from obstructions
- ☐ c. to show a driver what position to take when turning right

6. Are you allowed to stop in a yellow box junction?
- ☐ a. yes
- ☐ b. no
- ☐ c. yes, provided your exit road is clear

7. What is a skid? (you may choose more than one answer)
   - ☐ a. when wheels lose grip on road surface
   - ☐ b. when wheels lock
   - ☐ c. when car slides to left or right
8. Wearing seat belts would reduce the risk of death or serious injury by what percentage?
   - ☐ a. 50%
   - ☐ b. 10%
   - ☐ c. 40%
9. When towing another vehicle, what is the maximum length allowed for a tow rope?
   - ☐ a. 10 ft
   - ☐ b. 5 ft
   - ☐ c. 15 ft
10. Is a learner allowed to drive on a motorway?
    - ☐ a. no, never
    - ☐ b. on weekends and bank holidays
    - ☐ c. yes
11. If dazzled by an oncoming car at night, what would you do?
    - ☐ a. stop
    - ☐ b. look left and slow down, and stop if necessary
    - ☐ c. flash him back
12. When driving, you come upon a triangle placed upright on the road, what does it mean to you?
    - ☐ a. nothing at all
    - ☐ b. vehicle broken down, slow down
    - ☐ c. slow down and stop

13. What should a pedestrian do to claim priority at a pedestrian crossing (zebra crossing)?
    ❑   a. put foot on crossing and go
    ❑   b. walk out
    ❑   c. put foot on crossing, look right, left and right again, and when safe, cross
14. Driving along a road which becomes a dual carriageway ahead, what sign might you see?
    ❑   a. yield sign
    ❑   b. tuning fork
    ❑   c. stop sign
15. When may you overtake on the left? (you may choose more than one answer)
    ❑   a. never
    ❑   b. when traffic in front has signalled right
    ❑   c. when traffic on righthand lane is moving slower than traffic in left lane
16. What does a green light mean?
    ❑   a. proceed with caution
    ❑   b. go
    ❑   c. be prepared to stop
17. What is the main cause of skidding? (you may choose more than one answer)
    ❑   a. driver
    ❑   b. bad tyres
    ❑   c. conditions
18. What is meant by the word "coasting"?
    ❑   a. driving with no gas (accelerator)
    ❑   b. driving with clutch up
    ❑   c. driving with clutch depressed

19. What is the sequence of traffic lights?

   ☐   a. amber/green/red/amber

   ☐   b. green/amber/red/green

   ☐   c. amber/green/amber/red

20. When stopping your vehicle, what control should you use first?

   ☐   a. clutch and brake simultaneously

   ☐   b. clutch first, then brake

   ☐   c. brake first, then clutch

21. Why is a yield sign so shaped? (you may choose more than one answer)

   ☐   a. internationally known

   ☐   b. if defaced you will know the sign

   ☐   c. you must stop

22. Are bus lanes only used by buses? (within times indicated)

   ☐   a. No, by buses, taxis and cyclists

   ☐   b. Yes, buses only

   ☐   c. No, by everybody

23. Which way should you look at a junction before entering another road?

   ☐   a. left/right/left as often as necessary

   ☐   b. right/left/right as often as necessary

   ☐   c. take effective observation

24. What is the national speed limit?

   ☐   a. 55mph

   ☐   b. 60mph or 96 km

   ☐   c. 50mph

25. Is wearing a seat belt obligatory?

   ☐   a. yes, with some exceptions

   ☐   b. yes, always

   ☐   c. no

26. At a stop sign, must you stop?

- ☐ a. always, yes
- ☐ b. not if you can see and nobody is there
- ☐ c. you yield

27. May you cross a continuous white line down the centre of a road? (you may choose more than one answer)

- ☐ a. never except in case of obstruction
- ☐ b. when there is a broken white line on your side
- ☐ c. on weekends and bank holidays

28. What position should you take when driving along the road?

- ☐ a. as close as practicable to the left
- ☐ b. along centre line in middle of road
- ☐ c. 1 ft from lefthand kerb

29. How do you turn right from a main road to minor road?

- ☐ a. turn at start of corner
- ☐ b. line the front of your car to the centre line of the new road and turn
- ☐ c. cut the corner

30. May you use bus lanes outside times indicated on plaque?

- ☐ a. yes
- ☐ b. sometimes (Saturdays and Sundays only)
- ☐ c. never

31. What should you do first on approaching a junction?

- ☐ a. reduce speed
- ☐ b. reduce gears
- ☐ c. signal

32. How would you recognize a zebra crossing?

- ☐ a. traffic signs
- ☐ b. flashing beacons
- ☐ c. stop sign

33. When starting to move away from the roadside, what should you mainly pay attention to?

- ☐ a. oncoming traffic
- ☐ b. blind spots
- ☐ c. pedestrians

34. When driving, what distance should you keep from the car in front of you?

- ☐ a. a yard for every mile per hour of speed
- ☐ b. 20 feet
- ☐ c. 3 car lengths

35. What shape and colour are warning signs?

- ☐ a. round, red and white
- ☐ b. yellow diamond shape
- ☐ c. square, white and black

36. Why is a stop sign so shaped? (you may choose more than one answer)

- ☐ a. internationally known
- ☐ b. if defaced you will know the shape
- ☐ c. it is a regulatory sign

37. There are two lines in the centre of the road: one broken, one continuous. When could you cross them?

- ☐ a. when the continuous white line is on your side
- ☐ b. when the broken white line is on your side
- ☐ c. never

38. What is the most effective warning at night?

- ☐ a. horn
- ☐ b. flash your lights
- ☐ c. sound your horn and flash your lights

39. What warning sign would you see approaching a roundabout?
- ☐ a. diamond (yellow)
- ☐ b. round (red)
- ☐ c. square (white)

40. When should you not use your horn?
- ☐ a. from 6am to 6pm - 06.00 to 18.00
- ☐ b. from 11.30pm to 7am - 23.30 to 07.00
- ☐ c. from 9pm to 9am - 21.00 to 09.00

41. What sign might you see first on approaching a main road?
- ☐ a. diamond shaped
- ☐ b. round shaped
- ☐ c. square shaped

42. What do two continuous white lines in centre of the road mean?
- ☐ a. oncoming traffic may overtake
- ☐ b. restricted vision on both sides, keep left, no overtaking
- ☐ c. to separate traffic

43. If you came across a continuous white line with a broken white line behind it, what would it mean to you?
- ☐ a. do not cross
- ☐ b. no entry
- ☐ c. drive slowly

44. At a stop sign with no stop line, where would you stop?
- ☐ a. at or before a stop sign
- ☐ b. at edge of road
- ☐ c. at side of kerb

45. Describe a stop sign:
- ☐ a. triangle
- ☐ b. 10 sided shape
- ☐ c. 8 sided shape

46. What procedure would you adopt when meeting a green arrow at traffic lights?

☐   a. proceed

☐   b. go disregarding arrow direction

☐   c. follow arrow only

47. Turning right on main roads, what procedure do you do first?

☐   a. signal/mirror/manoeuvre/mirror

☐   b. mirror/signal/mirror/manoeuvre

☐   c. manoeuvre/signal/mirror/manoeuvre again

48. What procedure and signal would you adopt when taking 3rd exit off a roundabout?

☐   a. drive in on right and signal left to leave roundabout

☐   b. drive in on left and signal to leave roundabout

☐   c. drive in on right, signal right on entry, give way to traffic, maintain right signal until exit before the one you want to take (2nd), mirror, signal left, manoeuvre left and leave.

49. On a dual carriageway what position should you be in waiting to turn right?

☐   a. in the central reserve, out of both fast lanes of traffic on both sides

☐   b. stop in fast lane with signals to right

☐   c. proceed and don't stop

50. When overtaking parked vehicles, what is the correct clearance to allow if there is no traffic around?

☐   a. 2 to 3 feet

☐   b. 4 to 5 feet

☐   c. as much as possible without crossing the centre line.

THE SELF TEST QUESTIONS ANSWERED

Did you know? (Answers to questions on pages 83-90)

1.	c.	**26.**	a.
2.	b.	**27.**	a / b.
3.	c.	**28.**	a.
4.	c.	**29.**	b.
5.	b.	**30.**	a.
6.	c.	**31.**	a.
7.	a / b / c.	**32.**	b.
8.	a.	**33.**	b.
9.	c.	**34.**	a.
10.	a.	**35.**	b.
11.	b.	**36.**	a / b.
12.	b.	**37.**	b.
13.	c.	**38.**	b.
14.	b.	**39.**	a.
15.	b / c.	**40.**	b.
16.	a.	**41.**	a.
17.	a / b / c.	**42.**	b.
18.	c.	**43.**	a / b.
19.	b.	**44.**	a.
20.	c.	**45.**	c.
21.	a / b.	**46.**	c.
22.	a.	**47.**	b.
23.	b/c.	**48.**	c.
24.	b.	**49.**	a.
25.	a.	**50.**	b/c.

Test Your Knowledge on Road Signs

Write in the meanings of these signs and fill in the spaces provided, in your own words, then check your answers on pages 102 – 104.

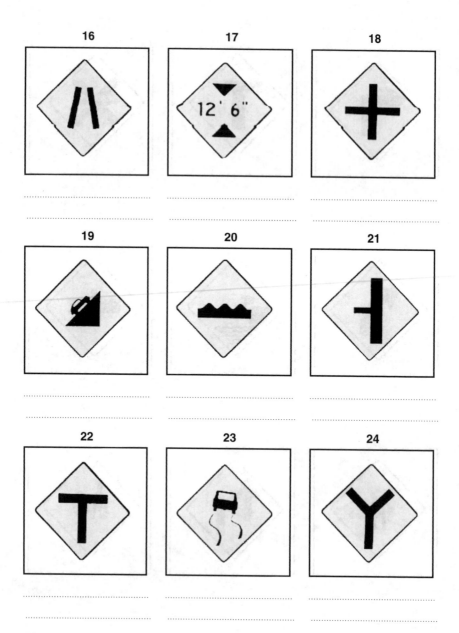

16 **17** **18**

19 **20** **21**

22 **23** **24**

25

....

....

26

....

....

27

....

....

28

....

....

29

....

....

30

....

....

IN CONDITIONS
OF POOR VISIBILITY
USE DIPPED HEADLIGHTS

Signs Giving Orders

Write in spaces provided. (answers on page 92)

31	32	33

....

....

34	35	36
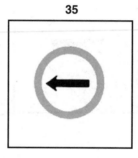		

....

....

WHEN IN DOUBT
GIVE WAY

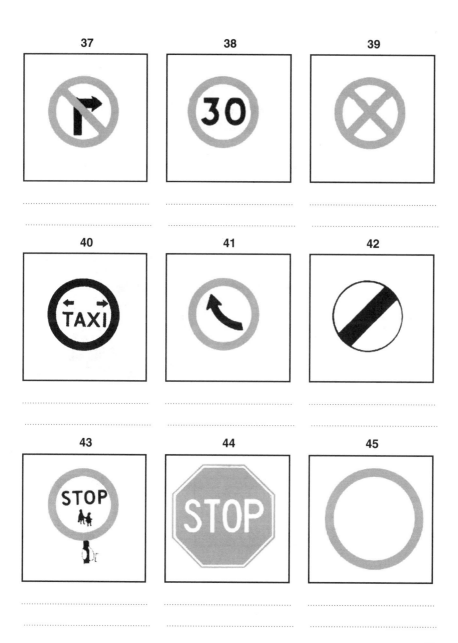

46

YIELD
RIGHT
OF
WAY

47

48

GÉILL
SLÍ

49

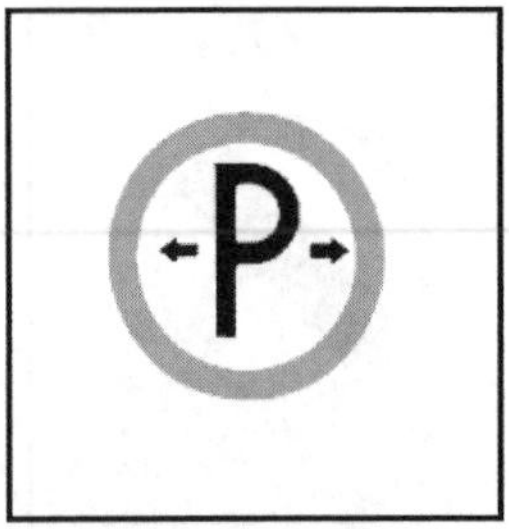

50

51

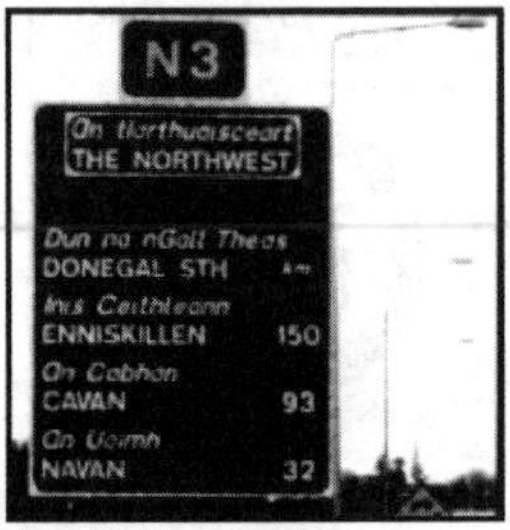

N3

On tUarthuaisceart
THE NORTHWEST

Dun na nGall Theas
DONEGAL STH

Inis Ceithleann
ENNISKILLEN   150

On Cabhan
CAVAN   93

On Uaimh
NAVAN   32

52

LOCH GARMAN
WEXFORD   2 | 18

53

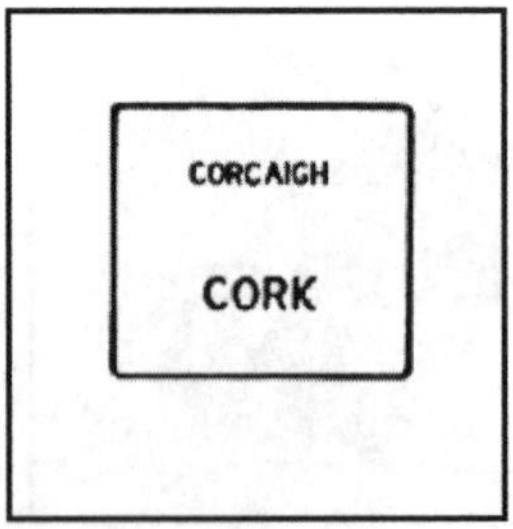

CORCAIGH

CORK

54

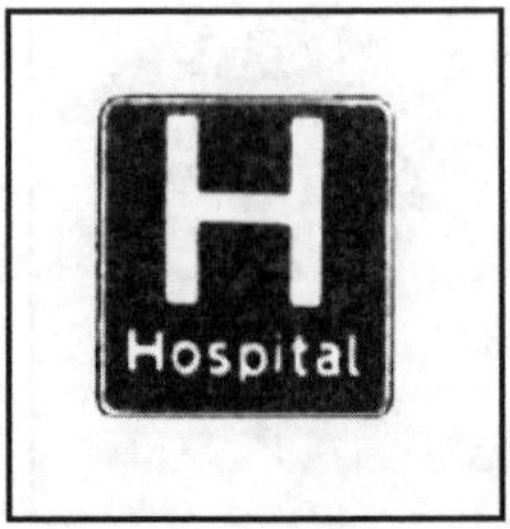

H
Hospital

55

56

57

58

59

60

KEEP LEFT

PASS RIGHT

Road Markings

(answers on page 102)

61

62

63

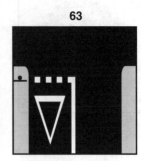

64

65

66

KEEP YOUR DISTANCE

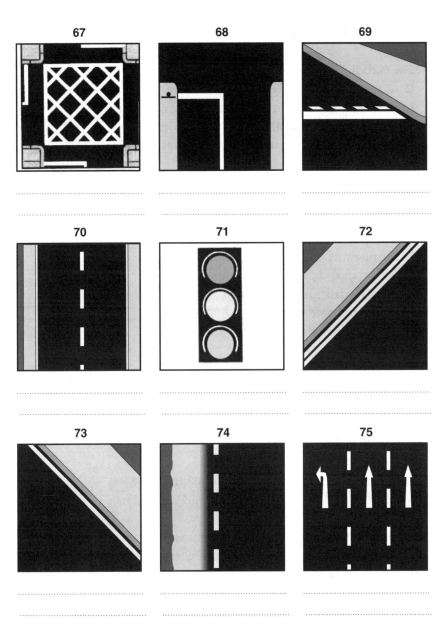

67

68

69

70

71

72

73

74

75

DID YOU KNOW?

Answers to Road Sign questions (pages 92 – 101).

1. Roundabout ahead
2. Junction ahead with roads of lesser importance
3. Dangerous bends ahead
4. Crossroads with roads of lesser importance ahead
5. Steep descent ahead
6. Sharp rise ahead (i.e. humpback bridge)
7. Dangerous turn ahead to the left
8. T-junction with road of lesser importance to the right
9. Unmanned level crossing
10. Dangerous bend ahead to the left
11. Unprotected quay or canal ahead
12. Major road ahead, vision may be limited and marked by a stop or a yield sign
13. Road works ahead
14. Dangerous corners ahead
15. School children's crossing
16. Road narrows dangerously or narrow bridge
17. Low bridge ahead
18. Crossroads with roads of equal importance
19. Steep ascent ahead
20. Series of bumps or hollows
21. Junction ahead, minor road, thin arm to the left
22. T-junction ahead with road of equal importance
23. Slippery road surface
24. Junction ahead with roads of equal importance
25. Staggered junction with roads of equal importance
26. Sharp depression ahead (road dips)

23. Slippery road surface
24. Junction ahead with roads of equal importance
25. Staggered junction with roads of equal importance
26. Sharp depression ahead (road dips)
27. Staggered junction ahead with roads of lesser importance (thin arms)
28. Junction ahead with road of equal importance
29. Major road ahead marked by a 'stop' sign or a 'yield right of way' sign
30. Level crossing ahead, guarded by gates or lifting barriers
31. Turn right only
32. No entry
33. Go straight ahead only
34. Do not park
35. Turn left only
36. No left turn
37. No right turn
38. Maximum speed limit 30mph
39. Clearway (i.e.: no parking within specified times)
40. Stopping/Parking for taxis only
41. Keep left
42. National speed limit sign
43. School Traffic Warden
44. Stop
45. No vehicles
46. Yield right of way
47. No motor vehicles
48. Yield right of way
49. Parking permitted
50. Motorway countdown markers (metres to next junction)

55. Cycle lane

56. Contra flow bus lane

57. Bus, taxi and cycle lane

58. Start of motorway

59. End of motorway

60. Motorway direction sign

61. Zig-zag lines at a zebra crossing

62. Areas of white diagonal stripes or white chevrons (hatchmarkings) are to separate traffic streams. Do not drive over these if you can avoid doing so. Where a chevron has a solid white line, do not enter except in case of emergency.
Remember: all solid white lines must not be crossed. A solid white line is a wall (except for traffic reasons).

63. Advanced warning of a yield right of way ahead painted on the road

64. Bus stop: no parking or stopping except for traffic purposes

65. Bus lane: you must not use the bus lane unless it is outside the times displayed

66. Road traffic lanes (directional)

67. Yellow box junction

68. Stop line

69. No entry markings

70. Central dividing line

71. Red at traffic lights

72. Double yellow lines: no parking

73. Single yellow line: restricted parking

74. Broken yellow line marks the edge of a carriageway

75. Traffic lanes

Conversion Chart

Use this chart as a guide to convert kilometres to miles and vice versa.

Kilometres	Miles (approximate)
5	3.1
10	6.2
15	9.3
20	12.4
25	15.5
30	18.6
35	21.7
40	24.8
45	27.9
50	31
60	37.3
70	43.5
80	49.7
90	55.9
100	62.1
110	68.3
120	74.6

Many vehicles, especially motorbikes have their speedometres in kilometres, not miles per hour. In the not too distant future, all road signs will be in kilometres. Some already are.

Motorcycles

Statistics show that four out of five motorcycle riders or their passengers, who are involved in accidents, are likely to be killed or injured, or to put it another way, you would be ten times more at risk than a person in a car. So, the importance of training is vital. Whatever about a car driver staying with the vehicle in the event of an accident, a motorcyclist has no chance!

Protective clothing and the obligatory use of crash helmets are also extremely important for driver and passenger alike. For all too many young drivers, buying their first bike will possibly be their first encounter with the control of speed. Before purchasing a motorcycle, a course of lessons should be undertaken. Check with your local County Council /Corporation Road Safety Section for advice on any training centres in your area or look in your local Golden Pages (classified directory) for a school of motoring, which instructs on motorbike driving.

A course should include:
- familiarisation with all aspects of machine control
- elementary road craft
- manoeuvering your machine
- handling of speed
- use of gears
- turning right and turning left
- use of brakes
- basic maintenance

The course should aim to bring your level to test standard and to teach you skills which you will use in everyday life out on the open road. These courses are certainly worth every penny spent. On average, fifty motorcyclists are killed each year in this country and many more injured. A trip to a hospital intensive care unit should convince anyone to take professional tuition. Always remember that professional instruction will reduce the risk of being involved in an accident.

You should always maintain your motorbike in good roadworthy condition. During daylight hours, drive on dipped headlights. Always wear a reflector belt and a dayglow jacket. Check tyre pressure carefully and regularly. Remember, if a front wheel blow-out occurs, you will have little chance of controlling your machine especially at higher speeds.

The importance of maintenance must be stressed: tyres, lights, brakes, chain, speedometer, indicators, steering, silencer, etc. must all be in working order to keep within the law.

Always make sure you have an up-to-date (current) provisional licence for the category of motorbike you are driving. If you are between 16 and 18 years of age, you may only apply for a Category A1. This licence covers motorbikes up to 125cc. If you are over 18 years of age, you may apply for a Category A. A provisional licence for Category A will only be granted to a person who holds a full driving licence for Category A1 for at least 2 years.

Note: the carrying of any passenger by a provisional licence holder is prohibited by law unless the person being carried holds a full licence for the bike you are driving and your insurance company allows the carrying of passengers. Remember, third party insurance does not cover injury to pillion passengers.

For further information on motorcycles, we suggest you read *This Is Your Bike* available through your local Licencing Authority. This book is also available from the National Safety Council, 4 Northbrook Road, Ranelagh, Dublin 6, tel (01) 963422.

MOTORCYCLISTS, SEE AND BE SEEN

ON THE DAY OF YOUR TEST

Categories A & A1 (Motorbikes)

- Make sure your vehicle is in roadworthy condition.
- Drive on dipped headlights.
- Wear a crash helmet.
- Wear a reflector belt and dayglow jacket.
- Ensure you bring your current provisional licence, valid for the category you are now being tested on.
- Bring your (valid) insurance cert.
- Ensure a current tax disc is displayed on the bike.

Without these requirements, the test will not be conducted and you will have to apply again for another test and forfeit the fee. As a motorcyclist, you need not display an insurance certificate or L plates while undergoing your test.

Procedure

You will be asked to sign a declaration of roadworthiness and the examiner will check the photo and signature on your current licence.

You will then be asked to accompany the examiner to your motorbike where you will be given some instructions and directions of the intended test route. After you move away, the examiner follows in another vehicle along your intended test route.

The rules state that a motorcyclist must be independently able to remove the motorbike from its stand, and walk alongside without the aid of the engine, and park the vehicle on its stand. The rules about the obligatory wearing and adjusting of the helmet will be examined. This may be visually checked, and you may be requested to demonstrate this and other safety devices on your machine. You will be asked to perform a "U" turn; keep the vehicle balanced at various speeds in different driving situations; demonstrate "lean over" to either turn left or right, whilst driving.

You will be asked to perform a hill start, then drive 50 metres at walking pace in first gear. The use of handsignals throughout your test is mandatory. The purpose of these manoeuvres is to show the examiner your overall control at a slow pace for manoeuvrability, balance and use of controls. After this, you will be asked to return to the test centre where you will be told if you have gained your certificate of competency or not.

HAND/ARM SIGNALS FOR MOTORCYCLISTS

Know the proper hand signals to give to other traffic. Hand signals, properly given, break the outline of your body and are easily recognised and understood. However if your motorcycle is fitted with direction indication signals use them as well as hand signals.

right turn   left turn   slowing down
or stopping

Keep the forearm at right angles to the body for clearest signalling, and make sure that your hand and arm are extended above hip level. Remember, when you are slowing down in order to pull into the kerb, give the slowing down signal - not the left turning signal.

Heavy Goods Vehicles (HGVs)

THEORY TEST FOR CATEGORIES C, D & E

The theory test for the Categories C, D, E and D + E will be on the same principal as for Category B but with much more emphasis on the items listed below.

To demonstrate knowledge and understanding of the following:
- obstruction of the field of vision of the driver
- the reasons that cause blindspots
- the effect of wind on the course of the vehicle
- rules on weights and dimensions of vehicles
- rules on driver hours, rest periods
- the use of tachographs
- the principles of the braking system and speed governors
- precautions to be taken when overtaking
- the reading of road maps
- checking the power assisted braking
- checking power assisted steering
- the use of the various braking systems
- the use of speed reduction systems other than the brakes
- adjusting the course of the vehicle when turning to allow for the vehicle length
- understanding vehicle swing and overhangs

Drivers of Categories B, B + E, C, C + E, D + E must know the safety factors of vehicle loading, and weight/load distribution, pertaining to their vehicle.

Drivers of the Categories B + E, C + E, D + E must be capable of coupling and uncoupling trailers and semi-trailers, to and from the tractor.

Drivers of Category D must demonstrate their knowledge of the rules concerning the carriage of persons, how to behave in the event of an accident, and know what safety precautions to take, e.g. cut off safety switches, etc.

SHARING THE ROAD WITH HGVs

Watch out for blindspots. Although trucks are equipped with up to six mirrors, it's still very easy for a car to be caught in a blindspot area. You should always avoid overtaking on the left handside especially close to junctions. When following a truck, keep your distance.

If you cannot see the truck mirrors, the truck driver cannot see you. Even if you can see a truck mirror, you may be in the truck driver's blindspot area.

Play it safe, give them room.

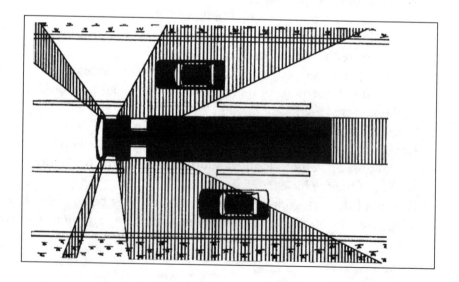

Area needed to corner

Big trucks need more room to turn corners so rear wheels won't mount the kerb.

Caution: Watch truck signals; keep back, especially if the truck is turning left.

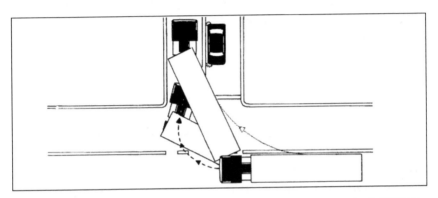

REQUIREMENTS FOR UNDERGOING A HGV TEST

A full medical for these classes is required, including an eye test for the following categories: C1, C, D1, D, EC1, EC, ED1, ED (reference D501 medical form). If you wish to undergo Categories C, D, D1, EC, you must currently hold a full licence for Category B or C1.

Light rigid C1 (over 3500kg but not over 7500 kg)
Minimum age: 18
Procedure: As Category B (see page 13).
Requirements: – A valid provisional licence to cover the category of test you are now undergoing – A valid insurance disc and tax displayed – L plates front and rear

Make sure your cab is clean and tidy, with all windows, mirrors and lights clean, and ensuring that all mirrors are properly adjusted.

Your test will last approximately 1hr 15minutes. Along the way, you will have to reverse into a limited opening on the left and into a limited opening on the right. You will be expected to move away safely and competently from a stationary position and on a hill (hill start), paying particular attention to the full use of all available mirrors. Check your blindspots. Along the way, pay particular attention to your mirrors when passing stationary vehicles and cyclists. Remember your maximum speed (see *Rules of the Road* for your category).

Truck C (over 9500kg)
Minimum age: 18
The overall wheel base must be not less than 3.75 metres from the centre of the front wheel to the centre of the back wheel.
Procedure: As Category C1
Requirements: As Category C1
Your test: As Category C1
Your speed: As Category C1

Articulated truck EC
Minimum age: 18
Procedure: As Category C1, C.
Test time: 1hr 30 minutes
Speed: As per *Rules of the Road*

Truck and trailer EC
Minimum age: 18
Minimum overall length: 12 metres

Rigid truck and trailer

Procedure: As C1, C, EC articulated with the exception of the reverse manoeuvre. You will be expected to reverse in a straight line along the left and/or right hand kerb for approximately the length of your vehicle. Remember your trailer must not exceed the size of the drawing vehicle.

Maximum speed: 35mph (see *Rules of the Road*).

Lighting Requirements

Normal lighting requirements apply to all motor vehicles except motorcycles. However, extra requirements may apply to heavy goods vehicles.

A motor vehicle (except a motorcycle) must be equipped with:

2 headlights (may be white or yellow), 2 white side lights

2 red rear lights, 2 red stop lights, 2 red reflectors to the rear of the vehicle, registration plate lighting to the rear of the vehicle, directional signal lights which may be amber in colour.

All lights must be in working order and kept clean.

You may obtain a leaflet called *Lighting on the Law for Heavy Goods Vehicles* from your local motor tax office or from the National Safety Council.

Trailers

Trailers or semi-trailers of 1.5 tonnes unladen weight or over should not be used on a public road without first being registered and licensed. An annual fee is required and certain conditions for the markings of the trailer must be complied with. There are some additional rules: from 1986, goods vehicle trailers (exceeding 1.5 tonnes unladen weight) must be equipped with an under run (protective crash barrier) when the trailer or semi-trailer is used in a public place.

Combinations of a motor vehicle or a HGV and trailer(s) exceeding 40ft must carry a side marker light on the right handside of each trailer and 2 triangular reflectors to the rear.

Projecting Loads

Projecting loads of more than 3ft 6 must be marked in daylight hours by a red flag or a marker board, or at night by a red light and a red reflector to its furthermost point. A load projecting to the side more than 16 inches from the side and rear lights, must be marked at night by a light or lights displaying white to oncoming traffic (front) and red to the rear.

Rear and Side Markings

Rear and side markings must be fitted to all vehicles of over 2 tonnes in unladen weight or on trailers of over 1 tonne or any additional trailers irrespective of the weight over 11 metres or 56ft in length.

Side markings are yellow fluorescent and amber reflectorised stripes. Rear markings are red reflectorised and fluorescent stripes.

These should be kept clean at all times to achieve the benefit of their original intention, which is to be seen.

Vehicle Weights and Dimensions

Maximum Width: Vehicle (other than a large tractor or trailer): *8'2½"*
Large Tractor (over 7¼ tons in laden weight): *9'*
Vehicle or trailer with load: *9'6"*

Maximum Height: Applies to public service vehicles only: *15*

Maximum Length: Rigid vehicles (goods): *36'*
Rigid vehicle (public service vehicle): *36'*
Articulated truck: *49'*
Trailer: *23'*

Combination of Vehicles: Vehicle combination comprising large tractor and two trailers (may only be used outside built-up areas) *72'*
Any combination of vehicles which exceeds 54 ft in length must have the words "over 54 ft" marked on the rear of the rearmost vehicle in the combination so as to be clearly seen from a reasonable distance.

HGV Weights
The following are the maximum permitted laden weights:
You may use the above weights table as a guide only as EC rules

Rigid vehicles	Tonnage	Limit adopted by EC from …	Proposed Irish operative date for EC limit
2 axles	18 tonnes	1st Jan 93	31st Dec 1998
3 axles	24.4 tonnes	1st Jan 93	1st Dec 1990
4 axles	30.5 tonnes	1st Jan 93	31st Dec 1998
Combined vehicles			
4 axles	35 tonnes	1st Jan 93	1st Dec 1998
(Road train 36 tonnes – articulated truck 36 tonnes - 30 tonnes if tandem axle of semi-trailer is fitted with air suspension and double tyres with an axle spacing 1.6m)			
5/6 axles	40 tonnes	1st July 86	1st Dec 1990
Others include:			
5 axle articulated truck including tri-axle semi-trailer with steel suspension (40 tonnes from 1st July 1986 – proposed Irish operative date from 31st Dec 1998). Tri-axle semi-trailer with air or fluid suspension (22.89 tonnes from 1st July 1986 – proposed Irish operative date from 31st Dec 1998). With steel suspension (22.89 tonnes from 1st July 1986 – proposed Irish operative date from 31st Dec 1998). Sole drive axle (11 tonnes from 1st Jan 1992 – proposed Irish operative date from 31st Dec 1998).			

and regulations change all the time. For further information contact your local motor taxation office for the information leaflet RT 16 or direct from the National Safety Council, 4 Northbrook Road, Ranelagh, Dublin 6.

A comprehensive manual on the CPC Certificate in Professional Competence on road transport operations is available from The Chartered Institute of Transport in Ireland, 1 Fitzwilliam Place, Dublin 2.

Categories D and D1, buses, coaches and minibuses

The driving test will be conducted as for any other HGV driving test. However, in the case of a vehicle in the above categories, persons applying for a driving test must be 21 years of age or over. The above categories include minibuses, buses and coaches capable of carrying more than 8 persons.

Note: Before commencement of any HGV test of Categories C1, C, EC1, D, D1, EC, ED, ED1, your tester will examine your indicator and stop lights and the general condition of your vehicle. Also required are two external mirrors, left and right.

The type of questions for HGV would be as is included in this book, with possibly more emphasis on the lighting requirements, vehicle weights, vehicle dimensions, projecting loads, loading and unloading a vehicle, speed limits relating to your vehicle, rear and side markings, parking at night, air brake pressures, hitching and unhitching of trailers and the use of tachographs. Most of these may be found in the *Rules of the Road*. For all reverse manoeuvres, your examiner will get out of the cab and walk to the rear of your vehicle and observe. He would only intervene in a case of extreme emergency. Pay particular attention to following traffic during the reverse manoeuvre.

Small Public Service Vehicles (PSV)

Small public service vehicle licences are only granted to a full licence holder of minimum Category B. These tests are normally only conducted at certain times of the year. Further information on the next available test date may be had from your local Garda station. The test, oral/written, is based on your overall knowledge of the area you intend to work in, including local hospitals, hotels, places of interest, particular routes and shortest distances from A to B.

Winter Driving and Your Driving Test

The only time a test would be postponed by the Driving Testing Centre would be because of bad weather, for instance, frost, snow, fog or the danger of black ice on routes. It would probably be a good idea to ring the Driver Testing section, (the number will be on the receipt of your driving test fee (acknowledgement slip) for information as to whether tests are being conducted or not from your test centre.

However, if your test is postponed due to adverse weather

conditions, a new appointment will be made for you and you will not lose your fee.

The Department is not normally responsible for any loss incurred by you, i.e. the cost of hiring a driving school car for the test, cost of pre-tests lessons or loss of earnings. However, cases have been known where an examiner, without prior notification to the candidate, has not turned up for a test. The candidate should then have recourse through the Department for the hiring of a school car.

Suggestions for safer winter motoring

1. Have your vehicle serviced regularly.
2. Check tyres at least once a week and keep them correctly inflated.
3. Ensure lights are clean and all are working and that headlamp aim is correct. In daylight fog use dipped headlights.
4. Keep windscreen clean and wash bottle filled.
5. Reduce speed in snow and icy conditions and during the hours of darkness, and increase stopping distance - remember, "keep the safety gap".
6. Keep in correct traffic lane.
7. Obey traffic signs and signals.
8. Signal clearly and in good time.
9. Avoid harsh braking and acceleration.
10. Develop the skill of "reading the road".

If there is a 'skid school' in your area, you should take a course. The skills you would learn there would include how to handle a skid, what to do in a left/right hand skid, use of brakes and steering etc.

Hints To Help You Pass First Time

1. Study thoroughly the *Rules of the Road* and this book, *The Driving Test in Ireland,* and the *Questions and Answers Theory Book*. Go through the Questions and Answers section and the Test Yourself Multiple Choice questions.
2. Make sure you take the advice and tuition from a full-time registered professional driving instructor who would be dealing with cases like yours on a daily basis.
3. Take the professional pre-test at your driving school. Your instructor would normally simulate the role of the examiner, thus giving you a true feeling for your test and only correcting faults at the end of the pre-test with no other conversation in between.
4. Be fully aware of what the examiner will be looking for.
5. Do not take your test too soon. If you are not ready to sit the test, you should cancel it, giving enough notice so as not to forfeit your fee. A new appointment will be made for you at a later date. (see detailed information on appointment form p.15).
6. As soon as you receive notification of your test date, you should phone the driving school, especially for those wishing to use a driving school car.
7. You should be able to drive unaided, confidently and safely avoiding undue hesitancy along the way.
8. Be able to demonstrate all manoeuvres that would normally be requested for your category of test.

9. Speak yourself through your driving test mentally on the day, it may seem a bit silly, but to a driving instructor it is the first sign of an advanced driver.
10. Do not allow your nerves to get too much in the way of your driving. However, **nerves alone** should not cause you to fail your test.

Your first full licence

Having passed your driving test you will be given a Certificate of Competency. You must remember to exchange this certificate for a full licence within two years from the date of issue, otherwise you would have to re-sit another examination.

Renewal of full licence

As a full licence holder, the responsibility is on you to have your licence replaced within a ten year period after the expiry date shown on your licence. Failing to renew it within the specified time, would mean you have to sit your driving test again.

Exchange of a foreign licence

Ireland exchanges any licence from the European Community. However restrictions may apply from outside the EC. You may check at your local motor tax office for further details of exchanges.

123

The Responsible Licence Holder

Having passed your driving test, you now feel ready for any motoring challenge, a trip through the city, to the countryside, on the motorway or even renting a car abroad. You are now one of the many millions of licence holders, but are you responsible enough to keep it? Below is a graph showing you how you may rate on the open road.

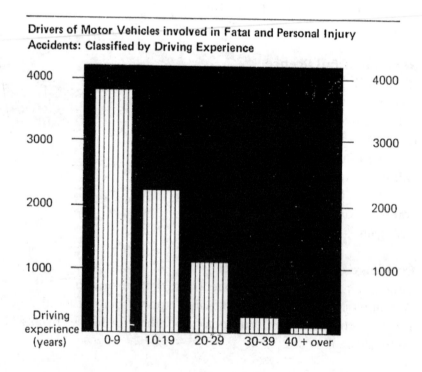

Drivers of Motor Vehicles involved in Fatal and Personal Injury Accidents: Classified by Driving Experience

To become a really good driver is not just a matter of gaining a Certificate of Competency. All that this states is that you drove to the required standard on the day of the test. Good safe driving always requires concentration, judgement, skill, care and courtesy. It is all about attitude, the right attitude, both to yourself and to other road users. Driving experience comes with time. Through this experience you will gain a knowledge which you will use in your everyday driving. As the graph shows, it takes approximately 9 years to become a reasonably mature driver. Between 0 to 9 years, speed is a major contributory factor to road accidents. Remember, always drive at a safe speed. What is a safe speed? The law states that a driver must be able to stop within the distance which he can see to be clear. Remember, test standard is a good standard to maintain for the rest of your life, it is not just for the day of the test.

What to do in the Case of a Road Traffic Accident

1. **You must stop:**
   See to any person who may be injured. You may also need to warn other traffic of the impending danger ahead. If injuries have occurred get someone to phone 999.

2. **Exchange information:**
   You must give your name and address, car registration and insurance numbers. If you are not the owner, you must furnish owner's or the company's name and address too.

3. You should ensure that you get the other parties name, address, vehicle registration number, their insurance company's name and address and their insurance number. Registration of insurance details must be displayed, by law, on the front windscreen.

4. **Witnesses:**
   Write down details of any independent witnesses' names and addresses or vehicle registration numbers whose occupants you feel may have witnessed the accident.

5. **Gardaí:**
   If any person was injured, you must call the Gardaí or if you feel the other party committed an offense.

6. **Admission:**
   Do not admit liability, even to say, "I'm sorry", may be taken as an admission of guilt.

7. **Statement:**
   You do not have to give a statement immediately to the Gardaí. Inform your insurance company first. You may well

be in shock and could incriminate yourself by doing so. Also, do not sign anything.

8. **Details:**

Take down any details regarding the scene of the accident e.g. wet or dry conditions, good or bad visibility, was street lighting working, were traffic lights working, travelling speed of vehicle on impact and the name and number of the Garda at the scene of the accident.

9. **Well being:**

If at all possible, do not drive soon after an accident. You may well be in shock.

Name: ....

Address: ....

....

....

Vehicle registration number: ....

Vehicle insurance number: ....

Insurance company: ....

Date: ....

Time: ....

Witness' name: ....

Address: ....

....

....

Witness' name: ....

Address: ....

....

....

Drinking and Driving

Now that you have gained your Certificate of Competency, you must always remember your responsibility to yourself and to other road users. Over a 10 year period, 4,851 people have died on our roads, that is the equivalent of the entire population of a small town, like Fermoy for example, which has a population of 4,882.

Over a third of all road accidents are in some way or another drink related. The peak time is between the hours of 9pm and 3am, especially on Saturdays and Sundays. There is a sharp rise in the holiday months of August and December. The good news is that the message seems to be getting through. In 1984 there were 8,500 arrests, in 1994 there were 6,000 and in 1995 there were 4,800 arrests. Yet the accident figures show that 437 died in 1994 (with 131 alcohol related) with the younger driver dominating the alcohol related statistics with a massive 72%.

The safe way to deal with alcohol is simply not to mix it with driving or, as the National Safety Council says:

"KEEP DRINK OUT OF THE DRIVING SEAT"

Some facts to keep in mind

1. You would be 5 times more likely to have an accident with drink taken.
2. A drink driving conviction could mean a fine of up to £1,000.
3. A loss of licence for a minimum of 2 years is automatic for the first offence and will be increased for a second or subsequent offence. Jail is also possible for up to 6 months.
4. An endorsement on your driving licence would remain for at least 3 years.
5. You would also have to inform your insurance company of the endorsement and then your insurance premium would rise by at least 100%. You would be unlikely to get comprehensive cover for quite some time.
6. You will have to inform your employer and may lose your job.

Remember:

- Don't drink and drive.
- Never push drink on a driver.

Safety Belts

Wearing your safety belt

As a rule, safety belts of an approved standard must be worn at all times by drivers (except when reversing) and front seat passengers of:

- Cars
- Station wagons
- Other passenger vehicles with seating accommodation for not more than 8 persons, (e.g. certain minibuses)
- Light goods vehicles (up to one and a half tons unladen weight)

These are the categories of vehicles which, by law, are at present required to have safety belts fitted.

Except in the case of children the onus is on the passenger to see to it that he or she is wearing a safety belt.

The law further states that passengers in the rear of a vehicle must wear seat belts (where fitted).

The requirement to wear a safety belt does not apply in the following cases:

- drivers of small public service vehicles (e.g. taxis and hackneys)
- a person giving driving instruction
- driver testers while conducting an official driving test
- members of the Garda or the Defence Forces while on duty.

A person will not be prosecuted for failure to wear a safety belt if, within a month of the alleged offence, he/she produces to the Garda Síochána a doctor's certificate certifying that, on the occasion in question, it was undesirable or inadvisable for that person to wear a safety belt because of physical or mental disability or for medical or psychological reasons.

The law also permits a person alleged to have committed an offence to plead in court that he had a special and substantial reason for not wearing a safety belt at the time, or to advance particular circumstances, e.g. physical, mental, medical or psychological considerations, or the nature of the use of the vehicle at the time. An example of the latter could be a person engaged in "door to door" deliveries or collections.

Remember, however, that the onus is on you to satisfy the court.

Wearing safety belts won't prevent accidents but they may help you to walk away from one. The restraining effect of a safety belt reduces the risk of death or serious injury by as much as 50%. As many as one hundred lives could be saved every year with full usage of safety belts in the front and rear seats.

The safety belts most commonly fitted to cars are of the lap and diagonal type. There are two versions of this belt - the "static" type and the "inertia reel". The latter is more expensive but has several advantages:

1. it is exceptionally easy to fasten
2. it is self-adjusting to the wearer
3. it allows some freedom of movement
4. it reels back automatically for easy clean stowage when not in use

As far as "static" belts are concerned it is important that when fastened:

1. the belt webbing fits firmly against the body with no appreciable slack.
2. the buckle or fastening point is positioned at or below the hip.

The more up-to-date "static" belt, commonly called the "one-handed belt", is much easier to adjust and fasten correctly than the older types. Proper adjustment of the belt assembly is absolutely essential to gain maximum protection in an accident.

Belts which have been worn during a severe collision, as well as those which are frayed, cut or damaged in any way should be replaced immediately.

In the fitting of safety belts it is important that the vehicle manufacturer's instructions as well as those of the belt manufacturer should be rigidly adhered to.

The maximum fine for not wearing a safety belt is £150.

Few people seem to realise the forces which are unleashed when a car is involved in a collision. If you collide unbelted with a stationary object at 30mph, for example, the result could be compared with falling out of a third storey window. Few of us would be simple-minded enough to try that one but some of us appear willing enough to risk it regularly in a car, despite the fact that most collisions occur at speeds of 20mph or less and within 5 miles of home. And, remember, no matter how experienced you are, or how defensively you drive, you have no control over the other driver - it doesn't have to be your fault to have an accident.

Travel Tips For Travelling With Children

When transporting children, never allow them to wander around your vehicle or stand on the seats, etc. It will never cease to amaze me to see parents allowing their children loose in a vehicle when they usually give them the best in life they can afford. Yet, no consideration is given to their precious little lives. Children trust you. The damage that can be done, even at 30mph or less, when your car stops suddenly and your child doesn't, is horrific. Some parents would argue: "I'm only going around the corner". But as statistics would have it, most accidents happen reasonably close to home. So, why take a risk? Belt them in, restrain your children, keep them safe and alive.

Prepare well for a journey with children. Whether it be toys, food, games or story tapes, the main consideration is to ensure that they do not get so troublesome so as to distract the driver unduly from his/her task of getting safely and comfortably to their destination.

On long journeys with children, stop every 2 hours or less and allow them to get out and stretch their legs. Bring along some of their favourite toys or maybe a security blanket if they use one. Remember, in a car the environment will be much warmer. Don't

NEVER

Never let a child sit on your lap in the front seat, even if you are wearing a seat belt. Children are far safer in the back. If they are old enough to sit in the front they must wear a seat belt.

NEVER

Never let a child stand on the floor or the seat while the car is moving. A sudden stop or jolt can cause serious injuries. Do not let him put his head out of the sun roof or out of the window.

NEVER

Never let a child put a hand out of the window. Not only is this dangerous for the child, but other drivers may think you are signalling and this could lead to an accident.

ALWAYS

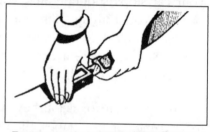

Remember: Fasten your own seat belt before you drive off.

ALWAYS USE A CHILD SEAT OR A BOOSTER CUSHION FOR CHILDREN

dress your children for an outside temperature. Ensure proper ventilation. If you smoke, try not to do so in the car.

Important notes

- Never leave your child unattended in your car, even for a moment.
- Never leave loose or sharp objects around the car because they may cause injury with sudden braking.
- Most cars have a child proof lock fitted to the rear doors. That

means, it cannot be opened from the inside. These are located beside the locking/closing mechanism of the door.

Myths

Possibly one of the most common mistakes people make about the driving test is to tell everybody about it. People who have already gone through it, seem to dramatize the whole operation. You will hear many stories, e.g. about quotas. This is possibly the number 1 myth "I did everything okay on the day, no problems, ah... his/her quotas were filled in for that day, so no matter how well I drove, I still would have failed". Another common myth is to say "Monday morning, ah you'll never pass, they don't pass anyone Monday mornings". I could write two pages on myths but I don't want to fill your head with any more nonsense. Others will say that the examiner was very disagreeable, fat, skinny, bearded, short, tall, he didn't speak, he grunted, left here, right there. Whatever the stories are, forget them.

My personal feeling would be that the fewer people who know about your test, the better. This way, you will not feel under any more pressure than you would normally be under on the day.

There are no quotas, no yardstick as to whether you will pass your test or not. Sorry, I am telling a lie. Experience, competence, confidence and capability will ensure you pass on the day. A lot of people take great offence to an examiner's opening words in the car just before you move off: "There will be no further conversation between you and me, other than to tell you to turn left or right. If you don't hear a left or a right, you may assume straight. You may move off when you are ready please" - agh, your mind screams!

Well, all of a sudden, the nerves start. Who is this person who was so nice for the administration section. Do not be unduly worried as he/she is instructed to say this to all candidates in the interest of uniformity, so don't take it personally. Could you put feelings into those words 8 or 9 times a day, 5 days a week, 48 weeks a year? If you have taken professional instruction, your driving instructor will have given you a good 'mock pre-test'. The silence in a car is something you will have to get used to, as your examiner, unlike the instructor, will not intervene, except in cases of extreme emergency.

Nerves play a very big part on the day. The tester will be understanding. By the first five minutes out, you should begin to settle down. Anybody would be nervous, an experienced driver even. Most instructors would agree with me on this point. When I get into a car belonging to a friend or colleague, the first thing they say to me is: "Don't comment on my driving, it is... years since I did my test". The fact is that they know they would not pass their test again (not without a professional pre-test at least!).

Remember

- Tell as few people as possible
- Ensure you are ready to sit the test
- Take professional driving tuition
- Read and study the Rules of the Road handbook
- Leave the nerves at home (if possible)
- Examiners are people too!

When you have passed, and you hear of somebody, a friend or a relative, about to do their test, keep the negative stories to yourself! Most if not all people would be nervous when undergoing a driving test. However, nerves may cause you to make mistakes. The important thing to remember is that one mistake should not lead to another. If you find that you have made an error in your driving, do not dwell on it as it may not be as important to the examiner at the time. Most examiners take an overall view of your driving. For instance, stalling your engine could be a panic moment for a lot of candidates. Don't panic, relax, immediately apply the handbrake and place the car in neutral gear. Start the car again. Apply first gear and move away again. Another typical one would be while waiting to turn right from a minor road to a major road. Waiting for your road to be clear may seem like an eternity with an examiner in the car. Last but not least, most people would say that the silence in the car is the worst, but remember, it is to your advantage as it gives you time to act and react to any traffic situation and is better for your concentration.

PROFESSIONAL TUITION PAYS

Road Rage

As a driver on our all too congested roads today, it is important to realise that we all share the same road space. As more and more cars join the road network, as traffic queues get longer and longer, with faster roads and motorways, there would seem to be less and less forgiveness for the mistakes of others. One should remember that the issue of a driver's permit is not a right, but a privilege and can be taken away for a proven case through the courts. It is with this in mind that we must avoid confrontation with other road users. Sometimes for simplest reasons, some motorists become irritated with others. Drivers should always be aware that attitude to other motorists and other road users is important. Never compete with other motorists, i.e. in speed or pride of place. Do not drive while stressed. Relax, or indeed take a walk before taking to the driving seat. Avoid tailgating the vehicle in front. Allow sufficient distance between you and others. Never cut in on another vehicle whilst driving or in a traffic queue. Never lane hop in front of another motorists. Always acknowledge a driving error that may have annoyed another motorist. Acknowledge a courtesy of another road user. Never allow your vehicle to make contact with another motorist, and never leave your vehicle if threatened by another driver.

Personal notes

Recollections of my driving test

Name: ....

Address: ....

....

....

....

Date of driving test: ....

Driving test centre: ....

Car used in test: ....

Test route: ....

....

....

Weather: ....

Result: ....

Certificate number: ....

Examiner's name: ....

Feelings after test: ....

Instructor's name: ....

Your driving school: ....

The price of lessons: ....

Personal notes

Personal notes